FORGIVEN AND FORGIVING

FORGIVEN
and Forgiving

L. William Countryman

MOREHOUSE PUBLISHING

Morehouse Publishing
P.O. Box 1321
Harrisburg, PA 17105

Morehouse Publishing is a Continuum imprint.

Printed in the United States of America
Cover art: Scala/Art Resource, NY. Guercino (Giov. F. Barbieri). *Return of the Prodigal Son.*
Cover design by Corey Kent

Note: A study guide for this book is available on the Internet at www.morehousegroup.com.

Library of Congress Cataloging-in-Publication Data

Countryman, Louis William, 1941–
    Forgiven and forgiving / L. William Countryman.
        p.   cm.
    Includes bibliographical references.
    ISBN 0-8192-1734-4 (pbk.)
    1. Forgiveness—Religious aspects—Christianity.   I. Title.
BV4647.F55C68   1998
234'.5—dc21   97-50258
                                                                                    CIP

03   04   05   06   07   08   10   9   8   7   6   5

In memory of
Robert C. Dentan
and
Pierson Parker,
from whom I learned both
scripture studies
and
faith

Contents

Why Forgiveness?

Forgiveness is a critical topic for our time—and a very difficult one. I don't know whether we find it harder to forgive than people of other eras or whether we just have more to forgive, but the inability or refusal to forgive has become one of the great destructive elements in the modern world, both for individuals and for communities. We hold grudges. We seek revenge. We cultivate victimhood as an identity. We let the past rule the present and future. We find ourselves trapped in anger, resentment, spite, dread, and hostility—emotions that poison both our own lives and our relationships with others. Time and again, our hope for peace is short-circuited by memory of past wrongs held dear.

How can we make progress in dealing with these problems? I don't propose a simple solution here, some step-by-step process guaranteeing that if you complete all the steps in the correct order, you'll be a forgiving person. I don't think there is any such magical solution. But there are ways of approaching these problems that can bear fruit over time in a new sense of who we are, a new orientation that focuses on the present and future rather than the past, and a new sense of generosity that makes forgiveness possible.

Accomplishing this would represent nothing less than a personal transformation for most of us. Whether as individuals or as groups, we tend to make war more easily than we make peace, to harbor or even treasure up the wrongs done to us more easily than we turn them loose. Transformations, of course, are always at least a little scary. To be transformed implies letting go of our control for a while in the hopeful expectation that something worthwhile can result. It means taking the risk that our old certainties might be replaced by a new way of seeing the world.

I don't wish to minimize or underrate the risk involved when we begin to seek the spirit of forgiveness. But I think it is possible to take that risk in reliance on God, who intends for us only and always good. It is a time in our lives to let God set the agenda, even though that's an unsettling step to take. It's a time for reevaluation and change—or, to give these concepts their more traditional names, repentance and conversion.

Here is an important and helpful insight about repentance, in the words of William Temple, a great spiritual teacher who was archbishop of Canterbury during World War II. I include his words here because they tell us something important about the leap we will be taking if we really want to become forgiving people:

> John [the Baptist] came, and after him Jesus came, saying, "Change your way of looking at life; the Kingdom of Heaven is at hand." But we have lowered the term "repentance" into meaning something not very different from remorse... Repentance does not merely mean giving up a bad habit. What it is concerned with is the mind; get a new mind. What mind?... To repent is to adopt God's viewpoint in place of your own. There need not be any sorrow about it. In itself, far from being sorrowful, it is the most joyful thing in the world, because when you have done it you have adopted the viewpoint of truth itself, and you are in fellowship with God. (William Temple, *Christian Faith and Life*, 67)

The pursuit of a forgiving spirit will turn out to be a matter not just of adding one more virtue to our stock but of being turned completely around and getting a new and forgiving mind.

Like me, you have perhaps thought of forgiveness primarily as a duty. But—let me be blunt—that's the wrong place to begin. Christianity, whatever you may have heard, is not primarily about duty—not about trying harder, doing better, tidying yourself up for the great banquet in the sky by and by. The word *gospel* means "good news," not "pep talk." However hard we have worked over the centuries to reduce Christian faith to a matter of rules (be neat, clean, and obedient; never miss church; say your prayers; read your Bible), it is really about something much more fundamental and life-giving than duty.

Christian faith is about the change of mind and heart that Temple wrote about. It is a change that will eventually affect your whole life, because when you see things in a radically different light, you can't just keep on behaving in the same old way, as if you still thought the old verities were all there was to be said. What we're talking about here is conversion, which means "a turning around." I mean "conversion" not in the relatively easy, simple sense of changing from one denomination or religion to another, but in the more difficult sense of turning around and discovering that there's a whole world out there that you hadn't really been aware of.

Conversion is nothing less than having our minds transformed according to the mind of God. By God's grace, we see things differently. And conversion—this new grasp of the world we live in—makes forgiveness possible for us. The point isn't to acquire a technique of forgiving or to drive ourselves harder through sheer willpower, but to acquire a whole new way of relating to God, the world, and one another.

Can we do this—make God's mind our mind—for ourselves? No, of course not. It's an intrinsic impossibility, like squaring a circle. To say "My goal in life this year is to acquire the mind of God" would be completely absurd. We can't make that happen to us. God is the only one who can give that gift. We can, however, be open to it, and we do that through repentance—the kind of repentance Archbishop Temple wrote about. As we think together about forgiveness in this book, we need to talk about it in the same way Temple wrote about repentance: not as a set of rules or commandments but as an opportunity to change our minds, our perspectives, and our vision of ourselves, our world, and God.

Forgiveness—
Not Quite What You Thought

⌘

What Forgiveness Isn't

If we are going to let ourselves in for the possibility of a change of mind, we should probably begin by looking at what sort of mind we bring with us to this topic. How do we conceive of forgiveness? What does it mean to us? For most of us, I think, our concept of forgiveness is a kind of muddle of several different, inconsistent, and inadequate notions. It will be helpful to identify some of them here.

One commonly shared misconception is that forgiveness is a matter of making nice. The motto of this sort of forgiveness is "They didn't really mean it." We think of forgiveness as a way to maintain the machinery of social interaction in operating order. To keep from disrupting it, we pretend that we have not been aggrieved by the behavior of others. We pretend that everybody's motives are entirely honorable, that everybody we deal with is basically good and rational. If people have in fact done us some harm, we assume that they didn't really mean it or that they were simply striking back at their dreadful childhoods and we had the misfortune to get in the way. We persuade ourselves that if others are treated with a little kindness, they'll all be perfectly nice.

As a means of social interaction, this way of thinking isn't entirely bad. If we confront one another constantly on every action that is less than perfect, we'll waste a lot of time pursuing the mirage of an unattainable ideal. Besides, none of us likes having our failings pointed out. We're more likely to get cooperation from one another if we cut each other a little slack. What is more, we can and do misread one another's motives. Sometimes actions that appear to be deliberately cruel turn out to have been merely thoughtless or inattentive. Sometimes what appears to be thoughtless or inattentive turns out to have been merely ill-informed or accidental.

It's probably also true that if we persist in expecting the best from one another, we are more likely to get it. We are more likely to rise to the occasion ourselves if we expect the best of others as well. Conversely, the assumption that everyone is out purely for number one actually helps create the kind of antisocial behavior that it takes for granted. Forgiveness as "making nice," then, may be a good thing if it establishes a basic undertone of civility in our social interactions. Assuming the best of others, not taking offense too easily, smoothing over the small, everyday collisions of life—all this has much to be said for it. If we assume that the other person "didn't really mean it," we'll be right much of the time. Not only that, we'll be creating a prophecy of good that tends to fulfill itself because it becomes the social expectation around us.

Still, it quickly becomes apparent that this kind of forgiveness has serious limits. It can deal with the small collisions of daily life, but it wears thin very rapidly when we are confronted with real and persistent wrongs in our experience. In those cases, we need a very different and more "real" form of forgiveness. Real forgiveness has to be based on something deeper than simple politeness. Ultimately, it needs to be based on "the viewpoint of truth itself." Maintaining a presumption of the goodwill of others is both polite and socially useful. But no matter how polite or useful it may be, there are occasions in our lives when it proves untrue.

If we are going to learn to forgive in these tougher moments, if we want a kind of forgiveness that is relevant to real life, it will have to be a great deal tougher than forgiveness as "making nice." It will have to start off by being completely honest, by admitting when people have behaved in a way that cannot possibly be whitewashed by our desire to see them as basically good and responsible persons. At some point, making nice has to yield, and we have to start paying attention and acknowledging how things really are.

Another mistaken notion of forgiveness is to make it a mode of denial, the forgiveness that takes as its motto: "It wasn't really that important." This is common, for example, in abusive household situations where the abused partner tries to minimize the harm done and to emphasize the perceived good of the relationship (however marginal or imaginary that may be). The abused person tends to think, "Perhaps I'm making too much of this. If I just accept it quietly, we can go back to the quieter times when everything seemed okay"; "He won't hit me again"; "She won't get drunk tomorrow."

Denial, unfortunately, usually turns out to be a bad idea. For one thing, it is usually wrong. Without some major transformation of life, the offender will hit again, steal again, be drunk again. Only a quite serious and deliberate effort to abandon old patterns and put new ones in their place is likely to change abusive behaviors. Usually, it takes not only some commitment on the part of the abuser but also a good deal of help from other people who understand how abusive personalities work either through prolonged study or because they have been there themselves and have emerged from its worst dangers.

Unfortunately, society and even the church often encourage this sort of denial, no matter how useless or destructive it is—and encourage it under the name of forgiveness. The abused person is urged to be long-suffering, to forgive the same offense over and over. This makes forgiveness appear to be a matter of putting up with the insupportable by making light of its real impact. "It wasn't really that important" moves from being an expression of hope to being an outright lie. In the process, harm is done not only to the abused persons but also to the abusers, who are never confronted in a compelling way with the meaning of their actions—actions that are destroying themselves, other persons, and their own relationships.

Can denial be a way of sharing "the viewpoint of truth itself"? No. When we speak of "the truth itself," we don't just mean God in the abstract, as if our knowledge or awareness of God bore no relationship to the rest of reality. If God is truth, then all truth is a means toward God and our relationship with God can be fostered only by truth. Lying, then, leads away from God. It can *only* lead away from God. Denying the reality of harm done to us is a lie, not a way of serving the truth.

Another way we distort and misunderstand forgiveness is by making it a form of emotional manipulation of ourselves or others. We think of it primarily as a feeling to be acquired by whatever means are necessary. How do we get ourselves to *feel* forgiving—or forgiven? How do we get somebody else to *feel* forgiving—or perhaps guilty, repentant, pliant, or whatever else would assist our project of winning forgiveness?

This is forgiveness as melodrama, a complicated competition for moral superiority based on who feels the right way and who doesn't. By forgiving one who has wronged me—and doing it with a certain public flair—I can gain and wield a considerable amount of psychological power over others. I can use my "forgiveness" to force the wrongdoer into public (and often insincere) repentance or to make the wrongdoer lose face by demonstrating my own nobility and long-suffering. I can use it to manipulate the audience into believing that I am without fault in the situation.

Conversely, the wrongdoer in the situation may use a display of penitence as a way to force the hand of the wronged party. By being extravagantly (and perhaps publicly) sorry, one may be able to force an act of forgiveness without having to do something more costly, such as make amends or reform one's behavior. Other people may be brought into the dramatic performance as emissaries, go-betweens, or a kind of Greek chorus to express public sentiment. Repentance can become a lever used to extort premature and unwilling (and often insincere) forgiveness.

I don't mean to say that the feelings involved in such transactions are unimportant or necessarily false. Nor do I mean to criticize all public penitence or every grand gesture of forgiveness. Forgiveness, as we'll see, is indeed a powerful act—an act full of power. And penitence can play a legitimate role in making forgiveness easier. But when the emotional transaction becomes the central issue, something important gets lost, for forgiveness is about more than feelings.

Our emotions are a tremendously important part of who we are. But forgiveness isn't simply about feelings; it's about how we live together, about how we undertake to behave toward one another, about the releasing of old wrongs, the restoration of peace, and the mending of relationships. If we tried to forgive purely by willing it or by thinking it without the involvement of our emotions, forgiveness wouldn't work. Moreover, the emotions, if unsupported by the rest of our life, are notoriously unstable. I can go right on feeling hidden resentment toward people years after performing such an emotion-laden, manipulative drama of forgiveness with them.

It may not always be others we're trying to control. Sometimes we manipulate ourselves into feeling that we have forgiven the other, and sometimes we manipulate ourselves into feeling forgiven. I think, for example, of a certain television evangelist who was caught in some embarrassing sexual peccadilloes a few years ago. Having retired from public view for a little while, he reemerged announcing that he had received assurance that God had forgiven him. Now, I firmly believe that God had indeed forgiven him—along with everybody else in the world. But my immediate reaction was, "Says who?! Why should I take your word for it?"

Alexander Campbell, a nineteenth-century preacher and reformer, used to point out that you can *feel* you are forgiven for some harm you may have done me, but the feeling doesn't really mean much. You only *know* you are forgiven if I tell you so. What made me suspicious of the television evangelist was that his announcement of his own forgiveness seemed to depend less on the word of God than on a certain feeling that he had acquired in prayer. Perhaps it was a genuine gift of grace, or perhaps it was a triumph of emotional self-manipulation. Who can say?

The problem arises when our *feelings* become the supreme focal point. If all we really want is to "feel right," then once we have manipulated our feelings into the preferred state, that's all that seems necessary. But real forgiveness—forgiving or being forgiven—goes well beyond that. It is a matter of getting a new mind, of having one's whole perspective on the world transformed and the behavior based on that perspective changed and made new.

Still another common misunderstanding of forgiveness treats forgiveness as a commodity. We purchase it by means of repentance—perhaps including penances that cost us dearly. This is the notion of forgiveness as second prize. First prize goes to those who do everything right the first time around. Second prize goes to those who repent really, really well. If you can't be perfect, you can at least be thoroughly ashamed of yourself, and that will earn a lesser reward.

But in Christian faith, forgiveness isn't something we *earn*. It's too late to earn divine forgiveness, because God has already given it to us as a gift. We may feel very deeply the wrong that we have done. We may feel the need to do some penance as an expression of our profound regret. Fine. Penance then becomes a means of making amends where possible, and a means of rehabilitation. It becomes an educational process in which we let the changed perspective, the new mind that is repentance, permeate our very being. But the penance will not earn God's forgiveness for us, because no one can earn a *gift*, particularly not a gift that has already been given.

Among humans, too, forgiveness is a gift, given out of the goodness of the giver's heart. For better or worse, you can't *make* anybody forgive you. If you manipulate people into feeling that they have to forgive you—or even that they already have—they still may not succeed in forgiving you from the heart. When forgiveness does come, it will be because the forgiver has found the interior riches that make it possible to be generous with the offender and the new mind that makes a person desire to do so.

When all is said and done, we are apt to think of forgiveness as a kind of complicated transaction between people that usually involves a good deal of misrepresentation, emotional manipulation, denial, presumption, and even outright lying. It becomes a formula to be invoked, an obligation to be fulfilled. Then, afterward, we sometimes wonder why we haven't really succeeded in turning loose our anger about the past.

We are perplexed because we *seem* to have done what we were supposed to do. We should forgive, shouldn't we? We're told to forgive by Jesus himself, so we had better just get busy and work on it and get it right, hadn't we? We'll do whatever it takes, from ignoring what other people are really doing, to denying our own feelings, to engaging in the melodrama of manipulation. And we'll feel that we're doing the pious, the religious thing.

But William Temple shows us a better way. Repentance isn't primarily about remorse, it's about the joyful sharing in the mind of God. What would forgiveness look like in those terms? How is forgiveness a way of sharing joyfully in the mind of God?

What Forgiveness Is

We'll understand the meaning of forgiveness best if we start off in relation to ourselves. Jesus tells us that God has forgiven us even if we don't seem to need forgiveness. What kind of way is that for God to deal with good, decent, respectable, religious folk? No doubt we have our faults, but they aren't that gross or dangerous. It would be nice of God to forgive our minor infractions—assuming that we've been appropriately penitent—but, really, there must be better things for God to do with God's time than to forgive people who don't really need forgiveness all that much.

Does that speech sound at all familiar? We think it, perhaps; but we wouldn't say it explicitly, even inside our heads. We know it sounds a little too much like the Pharisee in Jesus' parable of the two men who prayed in the Temple (Luke 18:9–14). This man (a particularly good and religious man, for that is what the Pharisees were) went to the Temple, the holiest of all places, to pray. He prayed a prayer of gratitude for his own goodness: "I thank you, God, that I am not like the rest of humanity: rapacious people, unjust people, adulterers—or even like this tax collector." (Tax collectors were considered very careless about religious observances.) The tax collector, by contrast, beat his breast and prayed, "God, be merciful to me, sinner that I am." Jesus then says to his audience, "I tell you, the second man went home with God's favor rather than the first, because everyone who exalts himself will be brought low, but the one who humbles himself will be exalted."

Jesus seems to like sayings about reversals. In another place, he says that the first will be last and the last first. Such sayings emphasize that God's favor is always a gift, not mere payment for our services. They also call attention to the dangers that lurk in self-satisfaction. Too much confidence in our own goodness can make us forget the common humanity that we share with every other person in the world. It's the kind of attitude that makes it possible for us to thank God that we are not like "those other people."

Because we remember Jesus' parable, we avoid reproducing the good Pharisee's worst excesses openly and aloud. Yet I think this prayer of superiority does rise up in our inmost souls sometimes in our relationship with God. After all, good, religious people of today, whatever our specific religion, are the Pharisee's direct heirs. We may not embrace his precise theology and spirituality, but we are religious people—devoted, responsible, reliable, generally solid folk. We can't help noticing that, can we? It wouldn't be truthful to pretend otherwise, would it?

No, it wouldn't. I'm not advocating another sort of lie, a false humility. In fact, there's a real value to basic moral goodness that it would be foolish to deny. There are people who do really evil things in our world. They cause plenty of pain and anguish. If the whole world were made of people like us, there's a chance it would be a better place. I don't want to dismiss that. Like us, the

Pharisees were not the worst people of their time, but the best. If Jesus found fault with them, it wasn't because they were bad but because they were good and they knew it; for there is a danger in that, too, as we shall see.

So why does God choose to deal with us by means of forgiveness? There are two reasons that are particularly relevant to our topic. One is that God's forgiveness undercuts the worst temptation of good people: self-righteousness. It saves us from getting stuck on ourselves in ways that can ultimately stifle our own souls and perhaps cause harm to others.

Remember the older brother—the good brother—in the parable of the prodigal son (Luke 15:11–32). When the prodigal returns, the older brother is out working in the fields (probably supervising the laborers, for this seems to have been a rich household). Coming back to the house, the older brother hears the noise of a celebration in the making. He knows that nothing was planned that morning. He can't imagine what is happening. He calls one of the servants and hears the whole story. When he has heard it, he's furious and refuses to go into the house.

His father hears that the older brother is outside, refusing to come in. He goes out to bring him in, just as he went to meet the prodigal brother when he saw him coming down the road. But the good brother resists. He wants to have his goodness recognized and rewarded. He's angry that his father is being so easy on the prodigal. The situation suggests that there's nothing special about being good and loyal all your life, that it makes no difference whether you've earned respect and honor or wasted them. The father says, "Your brother was dead and is alive again!" But the older brother isn't sure that's a reason to celebrate.

At the end of the story, we don't know whether the good son decides to go indoors and join the festivities or whether he decides to stay outside and sulk. Has he made such a sharp distinction between himself and his younger, more irresponsible brother that he can no longer see the two of them as linked; or will he choose to see himself as part of the family's restored and loving unity? Good question!

This isn't a trifling issue, nor is it purely an individual one. A sense of moral superiority can actually cut a person off from the humanity we all share with one another. In the larger community, moral superiority (or even the claim to it or the appearance of it) can produce chasms dividing one group from another. A sense of moral superiority can erect walls between social groups—or can be used to justify walls erected for other reasons. It can also be a tool or weapon to give one group an advantage over another.

Consider the ways we use moral superiority as a political weapon in the modern world. Some seek to claim this moral superiority by presenting themselves as "the virtuous people," the ones who can be relied on to abide rigorously by the requirements of morality. Interestingly, this often turns out to be a charade, with high moral claims being used as an effective cloak for dirty dealing. It's proverbial that the TV preachers who rant about sexuality often prove to be describing the very temptations they are giving in to themselves. And how many politicians who wave the flag of "family values" have proven to have family lives that won't stand up to inspection? These examples just confirm the prestige that the mere claim to moral superiority bestows. That's what makes it such a favorite ploy of the "religious" Right.

Another way of seizing the moral high ground is by claiming to be "the innocent victim." The claim of victimhood can be used not only to defeat the group that has victimized you but also to justify your own mistreatment of others. Because you have been a victim yourself, the assumption (both yours and others') is that you certainly wouldn't make victims of other people. You can therefore proceed to do so without detection—either by others or by yourself. This "moral" ploy is generally preferred by groups on the political Left, though the Right wing tries to exploit it, too.

The "victim mentality," which uses past wrongs to discount present ones, and the claim to special virtue, which cloaks the intolerance of the religious Right in the supposed virtue of a relatively established and conservative class, are two sides of the same coin.

It's a coin that has been used and continues to be used repeatedly in our times. The intolerance that self-assurance breeds, whether it claims victimhood or virtue as its source, can legitimately be called the principal social and political problem of our time.

Think, for example, of those film clips you have undoubtedly seen from the middle of this century featuring crowds of well-scrubbed young people with their bright and shining faces, their idealism, their commitment to high causes, their willingness to endure hardship in order to right the wrongs done to their country, their immense sense of their own moral rightness. I mean, of course, the Hitler Youth. They must, for the most part, have thought of themselves as decent, responsible, committed, respectable, patriotic people. They wanted to put right what they saw as the unfairness of the settlements after the First World War. They were attacking what they claimed was a great evil in the world as well as a threat to their own well-being and virtue. I suspect they managed, for the most part, not to notice that they were committing one of the great horrors of all human history.

We can still see the same kind of "virtue" creating the same kind of disastrous animosity in virtually every part of the world. Whether it takes the form of nationalism and "ethnic cleansing" in the former Yugoslavia or of religious fundamentalism and its efforts to "purify" society in Afghanistan; whether it is the politico-tribal bloodbath of Rwanda or the class warfare of El Salvador, self-righteousness turns out to have no conscience and no humanity. Virtue, when it begins to admire itself too much, turns out to be as dangerous to the world as the more obvious forms of vice.

There is a seldom-cited text of scripture that deserves to be taken more seriously in this connection. In it, someone writing in the name of Solomon rejects both extremes: "Do not be too righteous, and do not act too wise; why should you destroy yourself? Do not be too wicked, and do not be a fool; why should you die before your time?" (Eccles. 7:16–17, NSRV). The best thing is to know ourselves as we are—a mixture of good and evil. That will give us a sense of our common bond with one another, with righteous and wicked alike. "Solomon" would presumably not have made the mistake of the Pharisee in Jesus' parable.

For our own sake and for our neighbor's, then, we need to make a shift away from asserting our own virtue and relying on it as the source of our worth. Does this mean that public virtue is unimportant? Of course not. We need more honesty, integrity, reflectiveness, compassion, loyalty, and truthfulness in government, not less. But true virtue will add to these qualities the important gift of *humility*. True virtue doesn't waste energy calling attention to itself and does not stoop to using the appearance of righteousness as its principal argument in an election. The person who does claim moral superiority should be automatically suspect.

The consequences of self-assured righteousness run amok can be appalling. That alone would be enough to explain why God has chosen to deal with us not through complimenting and rewarding our goodness but through forgiving us. If God's love comes to us without regard to what we have earned, this undercuts the ugly misuse we make of our own goodness. Our basic relationship with God is based not on our merit but on God's generosity. Does that mean that virtue is bad? No, it just acknowledges that we need protection from our own misuse of it.

There's another important reason that God chooses to deal with us by forgiving us rather than by rewarding our virtues. Forgiveness gives us the breathing room we need to live and grow. If God's goodness to us is based on forgiveness, that leaves us room to make some mistakes in life—room actually to be human. I'm not *advocating* the making of mistakes; I don't need to, in any case. I'm simply recognizing them as inevitable. They are part of the way human beings grow and mature.

Which of us has been able to accomplish whatever is good in our lives without making some mistakes along the way? Often we have learned things from our mistakes and false starts in life that we could have learned in no other way. Human life seems to be constitutionally messy. It's part of the way we've been created. We are finite beings, without full, perfect comprehension. We feel our way through space and time as we learn and grow. There is no highway from infancy to maturity. It's all country roads with detours, dead ends, even places where we have to scout our own trail across untrodden country. The journey of human life and growth is an adventure, not an easy and predictable commute.

And there are places, of course, where we wander quite off the trail because we aren't paying attention or even run off in pursuit of something that, deep down, we already know is a mistake. The amazing thing is that even those mistakes become part of our path. As we emerge from our floundering in the brush, our wandering in the forest, and find a new sense of direction, we discover that we have not merely left our off-road misadventure behind. Instead, it has become part of us in unexpected ways. It has given us new insight, new courage, new humility, new life.

Perhaps it would be comforting, in a way, to imagine a human life that moved more nearly in a straight line, where we could see the goal from the starting point and where the road led directly from the one to the other. It doesn't sound too exciting, but it does sound more secure. We would be born knowing what it means to be a grown-up human being, and we would just keep practicing until we had it by rote.

But—for reasons best known to God—human life doesn't work that way. We acquire the sense of what human adulthood might mean only gradually—sometimes only in retrospect. We don't even begin with a perfect understanding of good and evil. If we did, all we would have to do is make up our mind to do one or the other. But in practice, we find that we have to keep thinking about good and evil all our lives, refining our understanding of them and recommitting ourselves to the good. God created us to lead precisely this kind of messy, adventurous, *educational* existence.

It might sound, in Genesis 2 and 3, as if we had found a way out. Wasn't the tree of the knowledge of good and evil the ultimate educational pill? Eat its fruit and you'll know everything. But human knowledge—at least our knowledge of ourselves and of similarly important things—doesn't work that way. All that the tree gave the human race was the ability to learn. In the ancient

Greek version of the passage, the tree is actually called something closer to "the tree of knowing what can be known of good and evil." What can be known changes as we grow. We can discern some things in advance, but not everything.

Forgiveness, then, gives us space to live and to learn, and it frees us from the temptation to credit our own goodness for too much. God forgives us because that was and is the most liberating thing God could do for us. It is the starting place for everything else.

Forgiveness and the Basic Structure of Reality

For the most part, we religious people tend to assume that the basic thing in life is commandments and rules: be good; do the right thing; love one another. We tend to assume that the world, or at least its moral side, is built on rules like these. And the rules *are* very important. They are worth taking seriously, both for our own sakes and for those of others. They teach us a certain beautiful order for life, one that respects the rights of others and seeks the well-being of the whole human race.

As I've already said, we'd all be better off in a world where everyone followed the basic commandments. Yet the commandments aren't central, either to God's inner life or to the world God has made. There's something more basic that undergirds reality, something that even the commandments depend on for their existence: God's love. God didn't create us because we were so good. We hadn't had a chance to be good. God created us out of love, the love that floods God's inner life and spills over into the work of creation. This love that began by creating us now goes on to reclaim us by taking the form of forgiveness. Like the father of the prodigal son, God constantly welcomes us home.

The message isn't a matter of "Be good! Oh, and by the way, God forgives you, too." It's a matter of "God has loved you and forgiven you. Now, what else needs to be said? How are you going to respond to that?" The only useful response, of course, is conversion—to take in this surprising reality and let it assume its rightful place at the center of your world. Jesus is calling us, through the message of forgiveness, *to change our minds.* If we do, we'll have a different notion of God and a different notion of ourselves as a result.

We may not necessarily welcome this idea at first. God says, "I love you right now, the person you are as well as the person you can become." We say, "That's all very well for you, but I have higher standards." Or God says, "I forgive you everything." And we say, "Go forgive somebody who needs it. I could give you a list." We resist forgiveness because we fear it will demean us. It will make too light of our hard work and our difficult virtues. Or it will treat our real faults too lightly. But God is not making light of *us,* God is making light of what bars us from living fully in God's love.

The message of forgiveness says to us, "Get over yourself!" Get over your goodness and your righteousness, if they threaten to keep you from full participation in your humanity. Get over your faults, your inadequacy, if they're what hold you back. Get over whatever it is that makes you self-obsessed, whatever makes you reject God's wooing of you, whatever makes you feel that you would rather not go in to the party, whatever makes you feel like you belong to some separate and superior race of beings, whatever makes you feel like an eternal victim, whatever keeps you from living a real human life, whatever makes you imagine that there's something in this world more important and more fundamental than love.

Instead, be loved. Why would you refuse it? Perhaps you do it out of pique because you think God isn't taking you seriously enough. Perhaps you do it out of shame and embarrassment because God is being kinder to you than you think you deserve. Either way, get over yourself. You are forgiven. Start there. In the whole universe, it is the only starting point there is, anyway. There is no reality deeper than God's overflowing love.

Here's a story about accepting forgiveness:

THE TWO DEBTORS

Two accountants worked for the same, very rich employer, and each of them independently used some of their employer's funds to speculate in securities. They didn't intend to steal the money, they just believed that they were very good at investments, and they expected to present their employer with a handsome profit by and by and to get praised for their good work. Instead, in the same market crash they both lost everything they had staked.

Both of them ran away. But they were people of principle, and they were very distressed by the way things had turned out. Each of them separately resolved to devote his life to replacing what he had wasted.

Through austerity, self-denial, and better investing, each of them finally succeeded in accumulating the needed amount. By chance, they returned on the same day, which happened to be their employer's birthday.

The first came in, made himself known, and explained that he was there to repay the money he had lost all those years before. But when the employer recognized him, he exclaimed, "Oh, that's right! That's who you are. But I can't accept the money. I forgave the debt years ago—only we couldn't find you to tell you so. You must come in as a friend and join my birthday party."

The man refused. He said, "No, I've worked all these years to pay you back. I can't think of myself as your friend until you have accepted my reparations. Otherwise, I'd feel like a hypocrite at your birthday party." He left and sat in the park across from the house and watched people going in to the festivities. He was angry, and his heart gnawed at him because his reparations had been refused and he felt he had been made light of.

As he sat there, the other man who had misused his employer's funds came past and went into the house. When he had entered, he made himself known and explained that he was there to repay the money he had lost all those years before. But when the employer recognized him, he exclaimed, "Oh, that's right! That's who you are. But I can't accept the money. I forgave the debt years ago—only we couldn't find you to tell you so. You must come in as a friend and join my birthday party."

The second man began to refuse like the first, saying, "No, I can't think of myself as your friend until you have accepted my reparations. Otherwise, I'll feel like a hypocrite..." But before he finished, he burst out laughing and said, "If you won't take this money back as reparation, then I give it to you as a birthday gift—and I accept your gracious invitation."

And the two of them went in to dinner.

Forgiving Oneself

Do We Really Accept God's Forgiveness?

Sometimes we think that we've accepted God's forgiveness of us, only to find that, deep down, we haven't. We have somehow bracketed it and treated it as interesting but irrelevant information. How can we tell? By the fact that we remain unforgiving of ourselves. It's all very well of God to forgive us, and we deign to accept the kindness, knowing that it is well meant. But we're not going to let ourselves off the hook so easily. We still reserve the right to have higher standards than God.

Sorry. It won't work. If we aren't forgiving of our own failures and errors, we aren't really taking God's forgiveness of us seriously, either. We're treating it as some bit of "spiritual" information that has no "real" effect on our lives. But this is God we're talking about—the Creator of all that is, including us. And still we're not sure that we need take God's forgiveness of us too seriously?! Do we think God didn't really mean it? Do we think what God does isn't really that important? Do we think *we* can take charge and do it better?

You see where we're headed here. We somehow manage to hear the good news of forgiveness without actually hearing it. It hasn't yet reshaped our worldview; we haven't accepted the change of mind that it implies. And so we're back again to where we started— at repentance, getting a new mind. It may take a long time and many encounters with God's forgiveness before we begin to take it with the seriousness it deserves and allow it to convert us.

Remember what we heard from William Temple: "Repentance... is concerned with... the mind; get a new mind. What mind?... To repent is to adopt God's viewpoint in place of your own. There need not be any sorrow about it. In itself, far from being sorrowful, it is the most joyful thing in the world." Forgiving ourselves is a matter of adopting God's viewpoint. It does indeed turn out to be joyful, but that doesn't necessarily make it easy for us to take the leap into it. Accepting a new mind is always a risky undertaking.

Embracing forgiveness turns out, strangely enough, to be an act of *repentance,* because it means giving up our own way of seeing the world and accepting in its place God's rather more generous way. This is true when we forgive others, and it is true when we forgive ourselves. Every act of forgiveness turns out to be a kind of conversion or repentance. And it is the most joyful sort of repentance imaginable.

All this emphasis on God's forgiveness may sound a little shocking. Isn't God just? Doesn't God care whether people do good or evil? Of course God cares. God cares because evil destroys people, both the people who commit it and those who become its victims. But God's notion of justice, unlike that of some humans, isn't focused primarily on punishment. It's focused on new life, on the creation of a new order of life for the world. God continues to desire life both for the sinner and for the one sinned against. God seeks an end to evil in the world, and therefore God forgives.

God has recognized—perhaps from the very beginning of creation—that love draws people more effectively toward the good than admonitions and threats can. There is a beautiful statement of this idea in a poem called "Discipline" by George Herbert, who admonishes (!) God to show kindness:

> Throw away thy rod,
> Throw away thy wrath:
>   O my God,
> Take the gentle path.

In the next two stanzas of the poem, Herbert points out that he is relying on the Bible itself in making such a request, because scripture tells him that God has already decided to do precisely what he asks. Then he goes on to praise the amazing power of love:

> Then let wrath remove;
> Love will do the deed:
> For with love
> Stony hearts will bleed.
>
> Love is swift of foot;
> Love's a man of war,
> And can shoot,
> And can hit from far.

At this point, you may already have guessed that Herbert is using the word *Love* as another name for God—a good biblical thing to do, since scripture tells us that "God is love" (1 John 4:8, 16). But lest the reader miss the point, Herbert gives an additional hint in the line "Love's a man of war," which echoes the biblical claim that "the Lord is a man of war" (Exod. 15:3 AV).

Finally, Herbert proves the power of love by reminding us that it persuaded even God to take a risk—to descend and become one of us in the incarnation:

> That which wrought on thee,
> Brought thee low,
> Needs must work on me.

If love could bring God to make the greatest of all gifts, it will ultimately lead the rest of us, too, to the kind of new life that God desires for us—a life characterized by an increasing intimacy with God and by our own fulfillment as God's human creatures. Love is all-powerful.

Forgiveness, then, is not just an end in itself; it's a means to something more. There is a story about Jesus staying in a house at Capernaum. The crowd is so thick that no one can get near him. Along come some people carrying a paralyzed man on a stretcher. Because they can't get to Jesus through the crowd, they go up onto the roof, tear part of it off, and lower the stretcher into the room where Jesus is. Jesus' first words to the paralytic are words of forgiveness: "Child, your sins are forgiven." But that's not the last word between them. It's a prelude to Jesus' saying, "I say to you: rise, pick up your stretcher, and go home" (Mark 2:1-12).

God's forgiveness, then, is not just a matter of saying, "OK, you did something wrong, but I'll let you off this time" and it certainly isn't a matter of saying, "OK, you did something wrong, but I don't really care." It's a matter of saying, "OK, you did something wrong. Now, where are we going to go from here?" Forgiveness doesn't wipe out the past. What it does is put the past into a new context, a new perspective. It asks, "How can this past wrong now become part of the ongoing history of redemption? How can it be taken up into a new hope and become part of a new creation?" Your sins are forgiven. Now, rise, pick up your stretcher, and go back to leading the life that you alone can live.

We need to accept God's forgiveness as something affecting our own lives. If we accept it only in the abstract, we haven't really believed it at all. And we can't really claim to have accepted God's forgiveness of us until we are willing to forgive ourselves for our past wrongs. If we hold out for higher standards than God's, we don't take God's forgiveness seriously. We think we know a better way. We are determined to earn our place in God's favor. Until then, we reserve the right to be both unforgiven and unforgiving.

How can we turn this refusal around? One important step in accepting God's forgiveness and in forgiving ourselves is owning up to what we've done wrong. In fact, as we come to believe that God has indeed forgiven us and is willing to go on forgiving us and working with us for new life, there's no further reason to hide or deny our own misdeeds. We can't move beyond the wrongs we have done until we confront them, and God has created a "safe space" where we can do exactly that. We won't be trapped in them. We won't be condemned by them forever. We can look them in the eye now.

Only by virtue of being forgiven can we afford to see ourselves as sinful people. We can even afford to see ourselves as finite, limited, sometimes stupid people. We can dare to admit that we will never get everything exactly right, since that's not how human beings are made. I'm asking us not to pretend that we're worse than we are—which is a useless and ostentatious bit of self-dramatization—but only to acknowledge that we are as we are.

Yes, I have done some things in my life that were stupid, other things that were merely unwise, other things that were careless, and even some that were downright hostile and hurtful. I have, from time to time, harmed myself and others. I don't like confronting that, but once I've accepted the new perspective of God's forgiveness, God's willingness to go on loving me and working with me and befriending me, I can take the risk. And if God is willing to forgive me and seek my friendship, why shouldn't I be willing to forgive and befriend myself?

Forgiveness or Perfection?

Someone may be thinking, "Wait a minute. This is that New Age I'm-OK-you're-OK stuff. Doesn't Jesus say that we're supposed to be perfect in the way God is perfect?" Yes, Jesus does tell us to be perfect. Let's think a bit about what that means. What is your idea of perfection—the kind of perfection that Jesus might be summoning us to? Is your picture of perfection a kind of sculptured or crystalline beauty, with every molecule locked permanently in place? Or is it the more haphazard and fleeting perfection of a handsome tree or dog or deer or flower?

Human perfection has to be more like the latter—the organic perfection that grows over time and is never absolutely without flaw. Human beings aren't born full-grown. Even Jesus had to grow "in wisdom and stature and favor with God and with human beings" (Luke 2:52). As we've already said, that kind of growth doesn't happen without mistakes and missteps along the way. In fact, that's how much of our learning takes place. Human perfection is messy perfection; it's trial-and-error perfection.

Our standard of perfection needs to be appropriate to our human reality. It's pointless to expect human beings to exhibit the regularity of a perfect quartz crystal. We couldn't do it, no matter how much effort we poured into it. It's unnatural to us from the ground up. And even if we could achieve it by some incredible feat of will, it would be an odd and unsatisfactory sort of perfection, wouldn't it, if it had to be maintained at such a cost? You don't imagine that it's an *effort* for God to be perfect, do you? If it were, God wouldn't be perfect.

Our perfection must be something natural to us. Even if it is an effort for us to attain, it must not ultimately be an effort to maintain. Our perfection should ultimately fit us like an old shoe. It will be a state of perfect humanness, not a state of stressed-out, pseudoangelic overachievement. Our human perfection is something we grow into. It's our true maturity. In fact, in the New Testament, the Greek word that we translate as "perfect" (*teleios*) really means something more like "mature."

If we look more closely at Jesus' call to perfection, we find that it actually focuses on something that may not have been central to our previous ideas of perfection—divine or human. It focuses not on being meticulously good or always in the right or unfailingly correct. There's not a word in it about inerrancy or infallibility. It focuses, rather, on love and generosity, even toward our enemies:

> "You've heard that it was said, 'You are to love your neighbor—and hate your enemy!' But I tell you: Love your enemies and pray for those who persecute you, so that you may become children of your father in the heavens, because he makes his sun come up over evil people and good and sends rain on righteous people and on unrighteous. For if you love those who love you, what reward have you earned? Don't even the tax collectors do the same thing? And if you welcome only your kinsfolk, what are you doing that's special? Don't even the Gentiles do the

same thing? So, you are to be perfect the way your heavenly father is perfect." (Matt. 5:43-48)

That's the perfection Jesus calls us to—an overflowing of human feeling, of human generosity toward one another. And that generosity isn't even something we produce on our own. We get it from God—from the ultimate, transcendent generosity that created us in the first place and keeps befriending us even when we don't particularly deserve it and goes on forgiving us time after time. Human perfection, according to Jesus, means sharing in God's extraordinary, forgiving generosity.

Forgiving the Wrongs We Have Done to Ourselves

Don't be afraid to apply God's lavish forgiveness to yourself. Jesus, citing the words of the Torah, commanded us to "Love your neighbor as yourself." Now, if you do a bad job of loving yourself, your neighbor is not going to benefit much from that formula. That applies to forgiveness, too. If we are to have the resources to forgive others, we get them from God's forgiveness of us—and we do that by forgiving ourselves.

Extending forgiveness to ourselves is not a simple matter. Some of what we need to forgive is wrongs we have done to ourselves, and some of it is wrongs done to others. Some of the harm we have done was intentional and some of it was simply the awkwardness of a limited and blundering self that learns as it goes. Some of what we have done is easy to understand and forgive, some difficult.

Let's begin with the wrongs we do to ourselves. Part of our sinfulness consists in the fact that we forget to be loving toward ourselves. Sometimes that takes the form of deliberately denying ourselves what we most need: rest, friends, freedom to enjoy, to create, to be what God is calling us to be. We get the strange notion that God is somehow pleased by the sight of people rejecting the good gifts of the world around them—gifts that God created to be

29

enjoyed. For a long time (since around the second century), Christians have tended to treat the created order as if it were primarily a problem or a temptation rather than a gift. There is something wrong with that. Self-denial shouldn't be the ordinary, everyday stance of a religion that affirms the goodness of the creation.

Sometimes, of course, we deny ourselves for some larger, overarching purpose. Jesus even encourages that: "If anyone wants to follow after me, let him deny himself and pick up his cross and follow me." But he goes right on to say, "Whoever will lose his life for my sake and the sake of the good news will be saving it" (Mark 8:34–35). The larger purpose must be a life-giving one. Mere self-denial for the purpose of punishing or depriving the self is wrong.

Sometimes we use high-sounding excuses when in fact we are denying ourselves merely out of indifference or because we have no real sense of how wonderful is this creature of God that bears the name "I." Sometimes we deny ourselves because we want to punish ourselves for perceived imperfections or unworthiness. Sometimes we act as if we alone in all the world were of no worth and deserved no kindness. (It can be very satisfying in a melodramatic kind of way, but it's really a rather arrogant and narcissistic little drama.)

Sometimes we reject and harm ourselves in less obvious ways, by substituting superficial and misleading goods for the deeper ones that the soul longs for. In a quantified culture, that's easy to do. We measure worth in currency. We may try to substitute possessions for the security of a quiet soul. We may try to substitute company for friends, detached sex for intimacy, information for reflection, career for life. The number of people who reach their middle years and suddenly discover themselves to be empty inside is a good index of how easy it is to substitute the minor pleasures of career or the shopping mall for the deeper pleasures of the soul and spirit—and also a good indicator of the fact that it won't work forever.

For all sorts of reasons and in all sorts of ways, we shortchange ourselves. Then we look back at some later time and think, "Why did I do that, and what do I have left to show for it all?" We may become angry with ourselves—or deeply sad. We become divided within, so that we are both victim and oppressor. If we remember God's forgiveness at this juncture, we shall try to deal as kindly with ourselves as God does. Otherwise, life can easily become a continuously renewed cycle of reproach.

This sounds bad enough, but there is a still worse option—to deaden ourselves so that we don't have to deal with those unpleasant feelings. We draw a curtain over our distress, blame others for our emptiness, and seek relief in distractions and drugs. The problem with that approach is that life loses its joys along with its sorrows. The mere shoving under or drugging of emotion seldom accomplishes much. In fact, rejected emotions have a way of coming back in poisoned form at a later date. It's better to acknowledge the ways we have harmed ourselves, even at the cost of some pain, and ask how we can move on to a kinder and more productive habit of life.

For we don't have to get stuck in the distress. God is still calling you into friendship. You are on your way somewhere. You've stumbled along the way? Welcome to the human race. The wonderful thing is that, through forgiveness, God is able to take even our failures and turn them into raw materials for future growth. Think of it as a kind of spiritual recycling. Nothing gets lost, ultimately. Through the miracle of forgiveness, even our failures become the means of our spiritual maturation and the foundation of a priestly ministry to one another. They give us understanding of one another's sufferings and uncertainties. They enable us to stand alongside one another in the presence of God.

They also give us, within ourselves, a new certainty of God's goodness. How many hymns celebrate precisely this experience of God's reclaiming us! John Newton's "Amazing Grace" is the most familiar, with its joyful cry, "I once was lost but now am found!" Another hymn by an anonymous author, begins:

I sought the Lord, and afterward I knew
he moved my soul to seek him, seeking me.

31

This hymn continues by casting us in the role of stupid, awkward, impulsive, wrongheaded Peter as he tries to walk on the waves with Jesus. He becomes afraid and starts to sink before being rescued by Jesus from the sea (Matt. 14:28–32):

> Thou didst reach forth thy hand and mine enfold;
>   I walked and sank not on the storm-vexed sea;
> 'twas not so much that I on thee took hold,
>   as thou, dear Lord, on me.

By the miracle of forgiveness, our stupidities and our sinfulness are reconstructed into evidence of God's love and therefore become gifts both for our own benefit and to be shared with others. Why, after all, is Peter the prime example of discipleship among the Twelve? Not because he was so strong and faithful, but just because he kept coming back. He is important to us not despite his foibles and weaknesses but because of them. His very absurdity is his greatest asset, because it saves him from crediting himself with too much. When we join in God's act of forgiveness by forgiving our own wrongs, we are simply accepting God's gift and letting it go to work in us.

But remember that, to accept a gift, you may have to turn loose of something else. If your hands are full of your own longing to be perfect, if you hang onto the distinction of having higher standards than God, you cannot take hold of forgiveness. If Peter had kept on saying, "I'll do it myself," he would have drowned.

I realize that all this is particularly hard for the good church folk who are most likely to read a book such as this. After all, I'm one, too. We've worked hard to be faithful and responsible and maybe self-denying. We may even have had moments of success. But we are going to have to drop our pretensions and let ourselves be the rather ordinary, imperfect, human beings that we really are. It will be all right. The God who could love Peter and save him from the consequences of his own brashness can love anybody.

Forgiving Ourselves for the Wrongs We Have Done to Others?

Of course, we have also done wrong to others. What about that? Can we forgive ourselves in those cases? Do we even have the right to do so? Wouldn't it be presumptuous? Isn't it the business of those we wronged to give or to withhold forgiveness as they will? Isn't it our business simply to make our amends and wait?

Yes and no. Certainly self-forgiveness doesn't *take the place* of being forgiven by those we've wronged or of seeking reconciliation with them. It won't magically heal the brokenness of the relationships we've damaged. It won't automatically restore us to anybody's good graces. But it still has a role to play. Its role is to prepare us for the future.

Forgiveness doesn't mean pretending that a wrong didn't occur or that it doesn't affect the present situation. Every human act has consequences. There's no way to stop that fact except by stopping human existence altogether. If I forgive myself for the wrong I have done to another, I'm not pretending that the book is now closed on the matter or that there is nothing more to be done. Just the opposite is true: I acknowledge what I did and take responsibility for it, while also taking hold of God's forgiveness. At that point, I have no need to hide the past—or to hide from it.

When I forgive myself, I'm letting go of a certain kind of useless guilt—not the simple awareness of responsibility (that's precisely what I'm accepting and acknowledging), but a self-regarding and sometimes self-dramatizing guilt that leads nowhere in particular. While I hang on to this guilt, I am subtly presenting myself as having done something so terrible that not even God can forgive it. Although this behavior has all the external appearance of humility, it's really a clever and externally pious way of making myself the center of my own universe—the one person in all creation who is beyond the reach of God! There's a strange satisfaction in that. People can even linger in that state while remaining quite indifferent to the persons they have harmed. It's a guilt of no particular value to anyone.

By forgiving ourselves, then, we are giving God the last word on the matter instead of ourselves. We step out of center stage, where God belongs, and acknowledge that others have roles in this play, too. In the process, we actually create the possibility of moving beyond the past wrong and the chance to participate in creating something new. We quit pretending we are perfect, and that, paradoxically, frees us to do our best by shedding the burden of useless, self-centered guilt.

Now we can proceed to make amends, in a way respectful of those we may have wronged. Where possible, we can also begin to restore relationships. Because we have accepted forgiveness, our approach to this task will not be distorted either by a desire to escape responsibility or by a self-centered guilt that is really more about *us* than about what we have done to others. We do not need to lie about the past, and we are not asking others to help relieve us of our own bad feelings. We are free to relate honestly and respectfully.

I want to stress the importance of doing this in a way respectful of those we may have wronged. Sometimes the return of the wrongdoer is merely painful to the victim and only compounds the harm. It's no good barging in on other people's lives to satisfy your own need for closure. Still, if it can be done in a humble, tactful, and undemanding way, there is often room to reach out to those we have wronged and to offer a process of renewal.

If the person we have harmed is beyond reach (otherwise unknown to us, perhaps, or dead, or likely to suffer unnecessarily from our presence), we can sometimes make amends for what we have done in a more general way through service to others. We do this not to earn forgiveness but because we have been forgiven. God's forgiveness gives us permission to build a new future out of our past wrongdoing.

Forgiveness is not the last word in any story but a new beginning that acknowledges the past and still looks forward. God is saying to us, "Come. I still love you. Let's go on from here." And we say, in response, "Well, if you can love me, I guess I can turn loose of my own fear and shame long enough to create something new and better with your help." Forgiveness opens the door to the future.

Forgiveness in Communities

I've been speaking so far about individuals, but what I've said also applies to communities. Communities may also stand in need of ways to forgive themselves. Old, unresolved wrongs can warp the life of a community—a family, a work community, a church, a city, a nation—for years. For the restoration of its health, the community needs to come to an acknowledgment of its wrongdoing and deal with the resulting shame, grief, and guilt. It needs to stand in the light of God's forgiveness and, in that light, deal with itself and its past wrongdoings, whether against its own members or against others.

Health can emerge only if the old wrong can be confronted. Naming the evil is vital—and typically very difficult. Often those of us less overtly involved pretend the wrongs were really someone else's doing. But in most cases, the wrongs that dog our community memories were committed with at least the passive consent of the majority. If we consented in this passive way, it's neither truthful nor helpful to claim that we were not responsible at all. In the meantime, those who took the lead in the wrongdoing often work hard either to claim that no wrong was done at all or to bracket the offense and treat it as merely a bit of interesting but morally neutral local "history."

How does forgiveness get an entry point here? Sometimes it comes, surprisingly enough, from the people who were wronged. In many cases, they, too, were and are part of the community. If they find the grace to forgive the community of which they are a part, they open the way to repentance for others by naming the evil without rancor. In this way, there is a hope of defeating the tendency toward denial and easy omission and thereby making the past open to the redemptive recycling that forgiveness alone makes possible.

But for a community to forgive itself in this way, there is also

35

need of wise leadership among those who did the wrong. The risk we feel as individuals in acknowledging our wrongdoing and our stupidity is compounded in a community. Only leaders who see the hope of resurrection in the process will have the courage to move forward with it. This is a quality of leadership that is regrettably rare. But how else is Germany ever going to learn to live with its history of Nazism? or the United States with its history of slavery and racial oppression?

Living in Forgiveness

Forgiving oneself means trusting God's forgiveness enough to risk joining in it, to risk forgiving ourselves in partnership with God. It's scary, because it doesn't sugarcoat anything. But it's enormously liberating, too. If we take the risk, we no longer need to sweep our old wrongs under the rug by ignoring or denying them. Instead, we repent of them. That is, taking hold of the divine perspective, we see our wrongs for the harm they really are—harm to ourselves and to others. And, by the same conversion, we take hold of the ancient and creative power of God's forgiveness, which has been waiting all these ages for us to join with it in building anew with the debris of the past.

In this way, forgiveness turns out to look not backward so much as forward. We learn from our mistakes and failures so that we can build better for the future. Our repented wrongs may actually become gifts to share with one another, our forgiven failures a proof of God's love. We will not, then, be trapped permanently in the wrongs of the past, but freed to build better and more effectively.

As a result, we can offer ourselves, humbly and respectfully, to those whom we may have wronged, in the hope that relationships can be restored and made fruitful. There is, after all, no past free of wrongs. If the wrongs are allowed to paralyze us, there will be no future at all worth mentioning. This is not an idle threat, as the twentieth century's history of vicious ethnic, racial, and religious hatred makes clear. The alternative to for-giveness, in our world, is increasingly likely to be death.

But there is more to be said for the forgiven life than just that it is preferable to the alternatives. The forgiven life, engaged in redeeming the world, in making old things new, in setting up the fallen and restoring what has dropped into neglect—this life is in fact a realization of the highest potential of humanity. The joys of Eden, simple and beautiful as they were, pale before the riches of the age to come, replete as it will be with a suffering that blos-soms into new life.

An old stone wall, with its lichens and mosses and ferns, its weathering and erosion, and the burrows that small animals have made in it—such a wall is often more beautiful and almost always more interesting than a brand new one with its fresh-cut stones still brash and unsubtle. That is true of human life, too, in a certain way. I don't mean that babies are not beautiful. I mean that a human life that has tried to protect itself from the smudges of existence, the accidents and uncertainties and fail-ures that are part of being genuinely human, seems barren and dull next to a human life lived boldly—even if it bears the scars of some misadventures.

Human perfection requires growth and change. It is a form of maturity. A life lived with joy, love, and ardor, even if it has taken risks and made mistakes, is more likely to reach a genuinely human perfection than a life lived too cautiously, preoccupied with minute calculations, anxious to do exactly and only the right thing always—and afraid to come face-to-face with its misdeeds.

The perfect human life is a life lived with delight, a life with too many spiritual riches ever to have an exact accounting of them, a life devoted to the receiving and giving of gifts, a life in transition toward a glorious and messy perfection. If your stan-dards are higher than God's, you won't like that kind of life. So repent. Get over yourself. Accept God's forgiveness and extend it to yourself. Then you will be ready to share it with others, too.

Forgiving One Another—
Opportunity or Demand?

⧜

Thus far, I have presented a picture of forgiveness as spiritual opportunity rather than demand. I have suggested that it isn't particularly helpful to look at forgiveness as a duty, that it will make more sense if we look at it as a way of becoming involved in the great work of redemption by which God brings in the life of the age to come.

Forgiveness begins with God's expressing God's love for us by forgiving us. God could, of course, have decided, instead, to recognize and reward our own worth—but chooses not to. That doesn't mean that God is indifferent to our worth. God rejoices with us in everything we do well, in every virtue we acquire, in every moment of growth and understanding. But God doesn't build the future on our good deeds. God builds the future on God's own generous forgiveness.

It also doesn't mean that God is indifferent to the real problems of sin and evil. God isn't saying, "Oh, forget it! It doesn't make any difference, anyway." Quite the contrary: God is profoundly sorrowful over the harm we do ourselves and one another. God envisions, for us and with us, a future characterized increasingly by love and communion with one another. Forgiveness isn't a way of condoning evil, but of overcoming it— maybe the only really effective way.

As I was walking one day with a friend, a clinical psychologist, we saw someone training dogs in a park. My friend said, "I wish therapy were as easy as training a dog. It's all about convincing them that they're loved; it's really the same thing." With human beings, as with other creatures, the assurance of love is the foundation of everything else that is good in our lives. Forgiveness is God's way of giving that assurance in its most uncompromising form.

Being forgiven isn't the last step in a process, then, as if being forgiven settled everything. We are constantly creating ourselves and our world, and the process is a gradual one. There is no magic that can instantaneously change who we are; only growth can do that. Forgiveness makes it safe to begin changing and growing. It releases possibilities that would otherwise remain locked away.

C. S. Lewis, in his little book *The Great Divorce,* has a good image for what's happening to us and in us. He presents heaven as more "real" than hell. There is regularly scheduled bus service between the two, but when people arrive in heaven on the bus from hell, they find that the grass hurts their feet. No matter how attractive heaven may be, most of them get right back on the bus. Only by becoming more real ourselves can we stand to live in heaven, and that won't happen in a flash.

If you're loved, no matter what, by the one who gave you life in the first place, what does that do to and for you? It doesn't create an instantaneous transformation, but it creates the opportunity to build something quite new—a new kind of life, a new self— in relationship with the one who loves you.

This isn't a requirement in the sense of a duty, something that someone else is forcing on you. Love is a gift. There is no quid pro quo; it's not something you can buy. But it does have consequences. Accepting it creates a relationship with the giver. Accepting love means returning love. The giving and receiving of a gift creates the opportunity for a whole series of loving exchanges.

God, of course, has given each of us many gifts: delights, talents, hopes, loves, a life that is uniquely yours. You may as well enjoy all the gifts God has given you. God won't be suspicious or jealous if you grow in wisdom and creativity and all the other human excellences. There's no reason, when you're loved this much, to lead a crabbed, starved, pinched existence. You might as well lead the most splendidly human existence possible—one rich in love, companionship, creativity, generosity, delight. Forgiveness doesn't wave a magic wand and pull this new life out of a hat, but it does open the way for you to create it as you live it.

You can't have a life like this by *taking* it. It isn't something to be seized and possessed. You can have it only by offering yourself for it. The difference between seizing it and offering yourself for it is that, when you offer yourself for it, you recognize that you don't have control of it, that it's not yours alone, that it is available to others, too. God gives the gift to other people as well. We can receive the gift in exactly the same way as they—and in no other way.

The Social Dimension of Forgiveness

Even though I started off here by talking about God's forgiveness of *us*, our relations with other people inevitably enter into the discussion. That's because human life is intrinsically social, even for people like me who seem to need a bit of hermit time, too. We were created to be social beings from the start. It's not enough for babies to be kept clean and warm and dry and well-fed; they have to be handled, talked to, included in the human circle. As adults we still need one another—as family, friends, mentors, teachers, coworkers, confidants, people to laugh with and cry with... the list of the ways we interact is endless.

So forgiveness can't stop with *me*. If I were the only forgiven person on the planet, what good would that do me? I might as well be the only human on the moon. I'd be embarked on this new journey, this newly possible life, entirely on my own, without companions. And that would be as bad as never having such a life at all.

According to the stories in Genesis, God knew at once, after creating the first human, that it was bad for us to be entirely alone. The animals proved to be good companions but were not enough by themselves. And so God created another human like the first—created human *society*—so that we would have one another to sustain and help us through our long travel toward true human maturity (Gen. 2).

This is why God chose not to forgive us on a one-by-one basis. God knew that wouldn't do us much good. God chose instead to forgive the whole human race at once—and assured us of that forgiveness in the gift of God's child Jesus. Paul put it this way: "While we were still weak, Christ died, at the right time, on behalf of irreverent people. Why, one is scarcely prepared to die even on behalf of a righteous person, though perhaps one would be so bold as to die for the good. But God confirms his love for us because while we were still sinners, Christ died for us" (Rom. 5:6–8).

It's all a little outrageous. It may even seem that God is inclined to overdo these things. But at least the message is clear! Not *because* we're good; *before* we're good. Big gesture. Meant for us all. No exceptions. Christ died for *irreverent* people, for *sinners*— and, yes, for the relatively pious and good, too. But you don't have to maintain a perfect, unsmudged record for God to love you. That's already settled. God does love you.

So I can't be the only forgiven one. God has forgiven everyone else in the same way and at the same moment as me. That's a fundamental reality I have to live with. God's forgiveness isn't available to me as a separate, private arrangement. It's available to me only as part of this big package.

This reality has consequences. If I want to withhold forgiveness from my neighbor, I'm effectively withholding it from myself, too. If I am willing for God to forgive my neighbor, I'm allowing God to forgive me, too. It's all or nothing, everybody or nobody.

Forgiving One Another

But there's still another dimension to forgiveness, isn't there? God may forgive my neighbor, but does that mean *I* have to? Well, the teaching of Jesus is rather insistent on the point. In fact, some readers may have been wondering when I was going to come to grips with the language in the New Testament that makes forgiveness sound like a duty as well as an opportunity. Now is the time.

Consider the Lord's Prayer, for example, which contains a

potentially alarming statement about forgiveness: "Forgive us our debts, as we have forgiven those who are in debt to us" (Matt. 6:12; Luke 11:4). Some ancient manuscripts of Matthew's Gospel make it a little more hopeful. They say "as we are forgiving" rather than "have forgiven," making our forgiveness dependent on our present rather than our past performance. But the passage is still daunting!

This is a very important text for Christians. Most of us probably pray it daily. We at least pray it with great frequency—enough so that we may have become only half-conscious of what it says. But it places forgiveness at the very center of our conversation with God—and in rather an intransigent fashion.

This isn't the place for a complete discussion of the Lord's Prayer, but it is worth thinking for a moment about the way the prayer is put together. It begins by celebrating God's name and asking for God's vision of the world as it can be (and will be in the age to come) to be realized here and now (Matt. 6:9–10; Luke 11:2). Up to this point, it makes no direct reference to ourselves at all, except in addressing God as "*our* Father."

Having prayed for God's reign to begin and God's will to be done, we then turn to our own basic, everyday needs, summed up in the symbol of bread (Matt. 6:11; Luke 11:3). That's the first petition that relates overtly to ourselves. The second is the petition about forgiveness. The prayer suggests that our need to be forgiven—and to forgive—is on a par with our daily need to eat.

As we pray for forgiveness, the Lord's Prayer lets us set our own standard for it. We ask to be forgiven to the same degree that we forgive those who have sinned against us. (The version of the prayer in Matthew 6:9–13 uses the language of "debts": we owe God something; others owe us something. Luke's version, 11:2–4, mixes the language of "debts" with the equivalent language of "sins.")

Finally, the prayer concludes by asking that we not be led into a time of testing, but that we be delivered from evil (Matt. 6:13; Luke 11:46). In a way, these are two sides of the same coin. We pray to follow and enjoy God in tranquillity and peace. Perhaps there is at least a hint, in the order of the petitions, that this tranquillity will follow on the gifts of daily bread and forgiveness, that these gifts make it possible. Most versions of the prayer (though not the oldest ones) then close with a doxology that echoes the praise of God at the beginning.

Now, what are we to make of the petition "Forgive us our debts, as we have forgiven those who are in debt to us"? It seems pretty scary. I'm not at all sure that I want God's forgiveness of me to be limited by the standard that I've created in my own forgiving of those who've wronged me. If I have forgiven over the long run, it hasn't always been quickly, easily, or with enthusiasm.

And the saying that Matthew's Gospel places right after the Lord's Prayer sounds even more intransigent: "For if you forgive people their trespasses, your heavenly Father will also forgive you. But if you don't forgive people, your Father won't forgive your trespasses, either" (6:14–15). This seems to move a step beyond saying merely that we set the standard by which we are forgiven. In this saying, God's forgiveness of us is entirely dependent on our forgiveness of our neighbor.

Also, there is the parable that Jesus told in response to Peter's reluctance to forgive:

> Peter came up and said to [Jesus], "Sir, how many times is my brother allowed to sin against me while I keep forgiving him? As many as seven times?" Jesus said to him, "I tell you, not as many as seven times, but as many as seventy-seven times.
>
> "For this reason, the kingdom of the heavens is likened to someone who was a king, who wanted to settle accounts with his slaves. And when he'd begun settling up, one man was brought to him who owed him ten thousand talents. And when the slave had nothing to pay him with, he ordered him and his wife and his children and everything he had to be sold and payment made. So the slave fell flat at his feet and said, 'Be patient with me, and I'll pay you everything.' And the master had mercy on that slave and let him go and canceled his debt.
>
> "But that slave went off and found one of his fellow slaves who owed him a hundred denarii. And he grabbed him and

throttled him and said, 'Pay me whatever it is you owe.' So his fellow slave fell to the floor and begged him, saying, 'Be patient with me, and I'll pay you.' But he refused and went off and threw him into prison till he would pay what was owed. So when his fellow slaves saw what had happened, they were deeply offended; and they went and informed their master about everything that had transpired.

"Then his master summoned him and said to him, 'Evil slave, I forgave you all that debt because you begged me. Shouldn't you have had mercy on your fellow slave the way I had mercy on you?' And his master was angry; and he handed him over to the torturers till such time as he paid everything that was due.

"My heavenly Father will do the same thing to you, too, if you don't forgive each of you his brother from your hearts."

(Matt. 18:21–35)

Jesus is not making it any easier for us. This parable sounds very threatening. Forgiveness here sounds very much like a duty—and not just *a* duty, but the *central* duty. For this teaching is clearly not something incidental to the larger message of Jesus as the Gospels have preserved it. It is a repeated emphasis that appears in significant contexts: in the Lord's Prayer, in a parable of the kingdom. Matthew even thought it was important enough to include in the Sermon on the Mount.

Now, what exactly is going on? I've been saying that forgiveness is a gift to us from God. Paul wrote that Christ died for us *before* we deserved it, not *because* we deserved it. Is this the "some restrictions apply" clause—the one that's read very fast at the end of radio advertisements? Is this the fine print God hoped we wouldn't bother to read? Does it mean that God's forgiveness is really limited and conditional after all?

Is forgiveness, then, really a matter of duty, after all—a duty whose dereliction will be severely punished? And what sort of duty is it? *Can* you, in fact, forgive everyone "from your heart" just because it's your duty to do so? Do human beings work that way? Many of us have long conceived of the Christian message as a series of demands and duties. One might wonder how it ever got the name "gospel" or "good news."

Our answer to these questions will depend on how we read the Bible. The Bible is an enormously complex and sometimes contradictory collection of materials written over a long span of time. Christians have found in it a great opportunity to hear God speaking with us. But that doesn't mean it is simple or completely straightforward. No one has ever managed—or ever will manage—to take every word of it with equal seriousness. We all have to figure out which elements we believe are more central and which ones less so.

For Christians, the center ought to be the *gospel*—that is, the good news that Jesus came to teach and to embody. Because I've written at some length on this elsewhere, I won't try to repeat it all here. But I want to emphasize that no reader can avoid having to make some decisions about what the gospel is. Those who claim that they don't have to or that their particular version of the gospel is self-evident are fooling themselves. It's better to make the decision in a conscious, reflective, deliberate way, in dialogue with the Bible itself. That's what honest, responsible study of the Bible is all about.

We have to begin by looking for basic principles. What is central to Jesus' good news? Is it a message of doom? Since when is a message of doom "good news"? No, a message that assigns us an impossible duty and threatens to punish with eternal destruction our inevitable failure does not qualify as good news. Why would Jesus' first audience have welcomed it? Why would people have kept on receiving it with joy in age after age?

The center of Jesus' good news was not and is not duty, but *gift*. That is certainly the way Paul understood it—as a gift given out of God's inexhaustible love to people who don't deserve it. When Jesus goes on to say that we have to forgive one another as well and that the forgiveness we give is the measure of the forgiveness we will receive, he is telling us not about a limitation on God's love but about a limitation on the way we take hold of that love.

If God's love were limited, God would never have risked the

incarnation and the death on the cross in order to become one of us and to woo us and to seek our love in return. If God's love were limited, it is hard to imagine why God would have created such fallible creatures in the first place. The question mark never stands beside God's love, which is unbounded. The question is always about the extent of *our* love—how far we are willing to risk responding to God's love with love of our own, how far we are willing to become a part of what God's love is creating in our world.

Believing that God forgives my neighbor is part of believing that God forgives me. We have already seen that we truly come to believe God's forgiveness of us only when we forgive ourselves. The same is true with our neighbors. We truly grasp the reality of God's forgiveness of erring humanity—us *and* our neighbors—only when we begin to join in the process and share God's work of forgiveness.

The process of forgiving our neighbors, then, is also a process of learning about ourselves and our relationship with God. The person next to you is another you, forgiven by God just as you are. The person in the world who has done you the most harm is another you, forgiven by God just as you are. How can any of us pray God to forgive us if we're not willing for God to forgive the rest of humanity, too? How can any of us accept God's free forgiveness if we're not ready for the rest of humanity to accept it, too? Jesus says, "You can't."

Dealing with Past Harms

But forgiving others is easier said than done, isn't it? I may be willing, in an abstract kind of way, for God to forgive those who've wronged me, yet I may still not be prepared to do it myself. Is forgiving others really even necessary? Why does Jesus push us so hard on the point? Aren't there cases where it would be wrong to forgive, sins that are too grave for us to forgive, whatever God may do with them? Aren't there people who shouldn't be trusted, who will simply use forgiveness as an opportunity to do the same or worse things again? Or what about the situation where the person who wronged us never asks for forgiveness, doesn't appear to care about it, refuses to acknowledge that he or she did anything wrong at all?

These specific problems are all serious ones and deserve some consideration. We'll take a closer look at them later in this book. The point for now is that, however much Jesus may insist on our forgiving those who have wronged us, we have to admit that that can be very hard to do—and may even seem like the wrong thing to do under certain circumstances. It's no good sweeping these things away as if they were minor concerns.

First, look at your own situation, quite apart from what the person who wronged you does or does not deserve. The first concern may be not what the other deserves but what we ourselves need. We can probably all agree that we need to do *something* with the wrongs that others have done to us—if only for our own sake. If we try to ignore them, they tend to fester in our lives and become poisonous.

William Blake wrote an astute little poem, "A Poison Tree," that captures an emotional dynamic that we all probably experience to some degree or other:

> I was angry with my friend,
> I told my wrath, my wrath did end;
> I was angry with my foe,
> I told it not, my wrath did grow.

The secret becomes an obsession. The poet goes on to tell of nurturing it carefully:

> And I water'd it in fears,
> Night & morning with my tears;
> And I sunned it with smiles,
> And with soft deceitful wiles.

At length the anger becomes a tree bearing poisonous fruit. The foe, tempted by its beauty, steals and eats it—and dies. The wrong that the enemy did combines with the poet's secret anger to produce a poisonous and fatal result.

Probably most of us can think of a few times in our lives when someone wronged us in a way that was particularly significant for us. Someone may have done us a quite distinct and measurable harm, physical or social or financial. Or the harm may have been something less tangible but still very painful: someone may have put us down in a way to which we were particularly vulnerable, or we may have been just a convenient object for someone's free-ranging hostility or arrogance. Some of these wrongs may have been quite profound and may go on causing us difficulty years and years after they happened. What are we to do with these wrongs if we don't want them to turn poisonous?

One thing that *doesn't* help is to lie about the wrong. It's no good saying, "Oh, it wasn't really all that big a deal. I shouldn't have gotten so upset," "Oh, it's all right—really. Let's just forget about it," or "Oh, OK, we'll give it one more try" (even though you don't believe for a minute that anything has changed). As Blake points out, lying about wrongs, pretending that they didn't happen, only makes matters worse. Lies come back in more poisonous forms later on.

It's also not very helpful to get depressed about it. You may know the routine: "What did I do to provoke that attack? Where did I go wrong to find myself in a situation like that?" Sometimes we act almost as if we were personally responsible for everything wrong in the world. I suppose it gives us the security of thinking that we're in control. But, of course, we're not really. We can't really take charge of other people's failures and wrongdoings. They have wills of their own.

No, the appropriate reaction when someone has done us wrong is to recognize and acknowledge what's happened. For some that means getting angry—openly and honestly angry, not angry in the pent-up, poisonous way. For others it may simply mean recognizing our sense of hurt. If you're out of practice with honest emotions (and a lot of us are), you may be slow to catch on at first. You may realize a week (or more) later that something really wrong happened to you. With practice, you'll be able to reduce your lag time. But even if it does take awhile, notice the emotions when they come. Feel them wholeheartedly. They are the place to begin.

Have you ever noticed how the psalmists wear their emotions on their sleeves? When they've been mistreated, they say so:

> I am poured out like water;
> all my bones are out of joint;
>   my heart within my breast is melting wax.
>
> My mouth is dried out like a pot-sherd;
> my tongue sticks to the roof of my mouth;
>
> Packs of dogs close me in,
> and gangs of evildoers circle around me. (22:14–16 BCP)
>
> They pay me evil in exchange for good;
>   my soul is full of despair. (35:12 BCP)
>
> Even my best friend, whom I trusted,
> who broke bread with me,
>
>   has lifted up his heel and turned against me.
>   (41:9 BCP)

And when they're angry, they say so, often by invoking curses on their enemies:

> Let the table before them be a trap
>   and their sacred feasts a snare.
>
> Let their eyes be darkened, that they may not see,
>   and give them continual trembling in their loins.
>
> Let their camp be desolate,
>   and let there be none to dwell in their tents.
>   (69:24–27 BCP)

Now, the psalmists' culture was very different from ours, and I'm not advocating that we copy it in every detail. But the Psalms do remind us that we can't deal successfully with problems that we refuse to admit exist. I'm not suggesting that hurt and anger are the ultimate response to the wrongs that have been done to us. It's just that we can't *avoid* these unpleasant emotions by refusing to feel hurt or refusing to get angry. It doesn't work. They sneak in some other way, usually in a form that's even harder to deal with. So the first thing to do in response to harm done to us is to acknowledge the reality of the situation—to feel the hurt, to get angry.

This may seem like an odd suggestion coming from a member of the clergy. Aren't Christians always supposed to refrain from anger? Even the psalmist says, "Refrain from anger, leave rage alone; / do not fret yourself; it leads only to evil" (37:9 BCP). Well, hurt and anger are undeniably dangerous things—like love, like electricity, like any powerful current in our lives. If they take control of us and we become prisoners of hurt or mere channels of anger, something has gone seriously wrong. We'll say more about that later.

But this is still the right place to begin. It's the right place because it's the honest place. Even if the reality is difficult to face and gives rise to emotions we would rather not feel, there is no shortcut that will avoid this process. We cannot deal with realities that we won't even admit exist. And once we truly admit that they exist, the emotions will indeed follow. This is all right. The God we worship is the God of truth. That means that our God is never served by lies. It also means that God *is* served by truth, that truth has a role to play in the redemption of all that is.

We may get some help from another biblical text—a kind of double text, actually, as it is a passage from Ephesians that starts with a quotation from yet another Psalm: "'Be angry and do not sin.' [Ps. 4:4] Don't let the sun set on your anger and give no room to the devil" (Eph. 4:26–27). Anger has its place—but not forever. This is a "sunset law" for anger. It reminds us that anger is useful only in specific circumstances and in limited amounts.

"Be angry" when that's appropriate. "And do not sin" with

your anger. It needs some term limit. It should not go on forever. If it does, you become merely a channel for it, a way for it to make its presence felt in the world. When that happens, you are giving room to the devil—to a kind of impersonal evil that seems almost to generate its own energy, quite independent of what we want. It's no longer your personal, chosen evil. It's merely using you for its own ends, which is the reason we call it demonic.

The same observation applies to our sense of hurt. Hurt is useful, at the beginning, because it tells us where we are, what has happened, how we are evaluating it. But if it takes on a life of its own, then we become the prisoners of a seemingly eternal sense of being abused and victimized. Our hurt begins to define us—far more than do our gifts and hopes and joys. We lose sight of all the more fruitful and hopeful definitions of who we might be.

The first step in dealing with past wrongs, then, is to feel what we have to feel—usually hurt and anger. We won't get beyond these emotions without going through them. But this is the beginning point, not the goal. If we make hurt or anger our last stop, then we're consigning ourselves to a kind of hell, whether it is the hell of eternally reliving the wrong done to us or the hell of a perennially unsatisfied destructive drive. Either way, we are in danger of coming to the point where these emotions are no longer simply our own truthful emotional responses to an event, but a kind of force using us to its own ends.

The way to nip this process in the bud—or to break out of it once it has begun—is to enter into the process of forgiveness. We may feel that we cannot do that as long as our negative feelings are so intense. But embarking on forgiveness is not simply a matter of the emotions. It begins with a decision we make about how we are going to deal with the past wrong and the emotions it has engendered. It is a decision to enter into a process. We can make this decision even when we are tremendously hurt or angry; and the process of forgiving will take up these emotions and transform them—something we need for our own peace.

Forgiving Others for Our Own Sakes

What the matter comes down to, then, is that I need to forgive others for the sake of my own well-being. If I refuse to begin the process of forgiveness, I will find myself locked up in the pain of past wrongs. I'll no longer be shaped and determined primarily by the blessings and opportunities of my life, but by the harm someone else has done to me. To that extent, I won't be free to build a generous and blessed future.

So how do we go about forgiving? It begins when we make a choice to forgive. But that doesn't mean that it's purely an effort of the will. I don't just make up my mind to do it and then resolutely ignore my feelings on the subject. That's not forgiveness, it's denial. Jesus tells us to forgive "from our hearts." In the language of Jesus' time, the heart was the place where you made decisions with your whole self. It doesn't mean the emotions alone, as it sometimes does with us; it means the emotions and the reason cooperating with each other to make decisions that you really can live with, decisions that can become a part of you. How can we forgive "from our hearts"?

Sometimes, of course, it happens easily. The person who hurt us seems genuinely sorry. We want a restoration of the relationship. Our hurt and anger have perhaps already given way as other concerns have occupied our attention. The forgiveness almost takes care of itself. In those cases, we hardly have to think about forgiveness at all. It's the more difficult occasions, when forgiveness doesn't come easily, that force us to ask questions and to seek help.

When forgiveness doesn't happen readily, what do we do? We may feel paralyzed. We would like to forgive. We may even, in some sense, have chosen to forgive. But we don't feel that we are making progress. In such situations, we can't force ourselves to forgive, but we can offer ourselves for it to happen. We can become involved in a process of forgiving that will eventually free us from past wrongs. How do we do that?

I know of four ways to cultivate forgiveness, and all of them have to do with changing our minds, with cultivating a new and larger perspective on the situation in which we find ourselves. We have said from the start that forgiveness is about getting the mind of God. It means taking the risk that, if we could see things even briefly from God's perspective, something better might replace our pent-up hurt and anger.

The first of my four suggestions is *prayer regarding the one who wronged us.* When we raise up others in our prayers, we are keeping them in our world. Even if they have caused us great pain, we don't erase them from our world. Instead, we retain whatever sort of relationship we can while the process of forgiveness proceeds. It may not be an ideal relationship, of course, but it doesn't have to be.

I deliberately said "prayer *regarding* the one who wronged us" rather than "prayer *for* the one who wronged us." Your curses may be a part of this at first; they certainly are in the Psalms. Keep praying the Lord's Prayer, too. It will be more than a little uncomfortable to be praying those words and also cursing someone with whom we're very angry. But it is better to suffer with that tension for a while than to pretend that we have come further than we have. In any case, God isn't fooled when we leave things out. God knows what is in our hearts—sometimes better than we do. Best to let it surface and deal with it openly.

Anger isn't excluded ahead of time, then. As the process of forgiveness advances, the anger will eventually wither. Even before that, our prayer can move toward being prayer *for* the other person. We can pray for the one who wronged us even while we are still hurt and angry. Perhaps we will do nothing more at first than lay that person in God's hands. Perhaps we will pray, in the venerable words of the Great Litany, for God "to forgive our enemies, persecutors, and slanderers, *and to turn their hearts.*" Perhaps we might eventually begin to pray for the other as we would wish our enemies to pray for us. But whatever you feel you need to say to God about these people who have wronged you, don't drop them out of your ongoing conversation with God.

My second suggestion for cultivating forgiveness is to *reflect on the universality of God's forgiveness,* the forgiveness confirmed for us on the cross. As we've been saying, God's generosity is so extreme as to seem almost excessive—a happy thing for us all! It falls on all alike so that there is no possibility of anyone being excluded—not even you or me. We have the privilege of holding back and refusing to accept the gift. But God doesn't hold back. God gives everything.

In some versions of Luke's crucifixion story, Jesus, filled with God's power to love, forgives even the people who are killing him (23:34). You and I may not yet be ready to be this generous. That's all right. Jesus does tell us to be perfect as God is perfect, but we are allowed some time and grace to grow toward that daunting ideal. We don't have to achieve it overnight. The point remains that God loved us all enough to forgive even death at our hands. As we reflect on that, we pray for God's help in learning this same amazing and powerful generosity.

My third suggestion is to *reflect on God's forgiveness of you.* Even if you are a much better person than the person who wronged you, that's not what your worth in God's presence is based on; it's not what God's love for you is based on. God, to be sure, loves every one of your excellences and rejoices with you in all the good that takes shape in your life. But God didn't wait for you to become admirable before beginning to love you utterly.

I don't mean to encourage the sort of false humility that expresses itself in such disingenuous speeches as, "Well, I guess we're all sinners and I'm probably, deep down, as bad as the person who did this to me, even if I've never done anything like this to anybody else. So I guess it's all right." You *may* be as bad as the next person, of course; you may even be as bad as the person who wronged you. But you equally well may not. The point is, that's not the point.

God's love is the point. It is what "brought God low," what brings God close to you. And it can bring God close to the person who wronged you as well. Even though God does not force grace on us, God courts us in the expectation that love can have an extraordinary effect on our lives. And it can. It happens all the time. People can be transformed. Perhaps you have been transformed in one way or another by God's goodness. Grant God the freedom to transform your enemy, too.

My fourth suggestion is to *pray for God to lead you into the future.* The end of the story that began with the harm done to you is still unknown; in fact, it's yet to be written. God may be able to see it, but we can't. And we move into the next episode of this story with trepidation, precisely because it's still unknown. Only confidence in God can give us the hope that we need to move forward. Because God desires for us what is good, we trust that even our hard experiences can lead to something of value.

The past, after all, can come to mean many different things over time. We always carry it with us into our future, but we can carry it with us in a great many different ways. Stumbling blocks sometimes become building blocks. Sometimes our past sufferings become the foundation of our future gifts. In any case, the book is not closed yet. We have more of it to write, more of it to live.

The gospel is the good news of transformation, of resurrection. As we seek to "get the mind of God," we can expect our new way of being in the world to look something like the resurrection. When the risen Jesus appeared to the disciples, he still carried the marks of his crucifixion—the imprint of the nails that fixed him on the cross—but they were transfigured by a new life and turned from marks of shame and suffering into marks of grace and glory. How will the remainder of *our* stories transform the marks of past wrongs into new life? That remains to be seen.

Forgiveness Builds the Future

O n the surface, it looks as if forgiveness is primarily about the past. We forgive something that happened in the past or someone who harmed us in the past. We talk about "forgiving and forgetting," about "wiping the slate clean." We may even envision forgiveness as returning us to point zero, as if the offense had never happened, so that we can begin again from the beginning.

There are dangers in this way of thinking about forgiveness. It encourages us to see forgiveness as denial. It seems to justify ignoring the past and pretending that it was and is of no importance. It can easily take us back to the wrong notions of forgiveness that I objected to at the beginning of this book, forgiveness as a kind of lie or a method of emotional manipulation.

In fact, forgiveness is not primarily about the past but about the future. There is no way of erasing the past, and we always carry our past with us into the future. The question is not *whether* we carry it with us but *how* we carry it—how we interpret it and how we build with it. Do we drag the past with us like a dead weight, a ball and chain, something that holds us back? Do we carry it as a kind of guilty secret, as something we don't want to give room to in the future and yet can't quite discard? Do we carry it as a weapon to use against ourselves or someone else? Do we carry the memory of past wrongs as a kind of shield to protect ourselves from the uncertainty of the future?

There is an alternative to these approaches. We can carry the past along with us as building material to create a larger and more generous future. We can see past wrongs, both those we have done and those done to us, as occasions to learn and grow and get a new mind. We can move beyond them toward reconciliation. We can play a part in God's great project of redeeming the past and creating from it the life of the age to come. The means by which we do this is forgiveness. Forgiveness is what turns past wrong into future possibility.

Forgiveness and the Future

We spoke earlier about God's forgiveness of us, about God's amazing generosity, about the way God showers us with forgiveness even before any repentance on our part. By forgiving us in this way, God opens for us the way to future growth in love. Along with forgiveness, God gives us all the gifts we need for building, together, the life of the future. Forgiveness, then, is the foundation on which God builds the life of the age to come. It may not seem the most sensible foundation to us, but God is, after all, the Creator of all that is and probably has some building skills. God might even know best in the matter.

The author of Ephesians makes exactly this point in describing what God was doing in the passion and death of Jesus:

> For [Jesus] himself is our peace—the one who made both sides [i.e., Jews and Gentiles] one and dissolved the wall that fenced them off from each other, the hostility, in his own flesh, and nullified the law of the commandments with its strict injunctions—all so that he might create the two thereby into one new humanity, making peace, and might reconcile both in a single body to God through the cross, having killed the hostility thereby. (Eph. 2:14–16).

What is this rather involved passage telling us? God was willing to endure death in Jesus to set going the process of forgiveness among human beings, beginning with these two groups who defined themselves as polar opposites of one another. The goal of this process is nothing less than a new creation of humanity.

Has this in fact happened? No. It *is happening.* It is happening every time two people take a step away from hostility toward peace. It can happen only in our own responses and relationships—not just with God but with the rest of humanity. God cannot make it happen unilaterally. God can only give it the opportunity to happen. It happens, bit by bit, through our own involvement in it.

Thus God chooses us by forgiving us, showers us with all sorts of gifts, and calls us to be... what? There are many images for that ultimate goal toward which God calls us, but one that I find particularly helpful is that of citizenship in the age to come—an age in which we human beings shed our need to do harm and live in peace with one another and with the world around us. This is our goal.

But this goal doesn't simply wait on some distant moment of future fulfillment. We are citizens now of the age to come—not perfect citizens, maybe, but citizens nonetheless. The question before us, then, is how we should live as citizens. How do we start to live the life of the age to come—that age which is our true home—in this rather difficult world of strife and uncertainty and failure, a world of pain and hurt as well as growth and new life? We are, in a sense, resident aliens in this world. More than that, we are a fifth column of the future.

If God has chosen to create the future through forgiveness and has even been willing to suffer in the process what we suffer in this world, then we might do well to join in God's work. By forgiving, we actually share in the life and work of God—we share in God's creation of the future. And to share in God's life means sharing in God's joy, too. Joy, not duty, is the ultimate appeal that draws us to forgive.

God certainly doesn't forgive us out of duty. What experience does God have of duty? God knows no "ought." God simply *is.* The forgiveness flows, then, out of God's abundant life. When we manage really to forgive others, it's because we, too, are participating in that life, perhaps in ways that we don't yet understand. God's love flows into us and through us and out onto others.

We are already citizens of the age to come, even if at the moment we seem to be living in some outlying and rebellious province. This means that even if we have not yet arrived in the age to come, we already live by God's joy. And by the power of that joy, we are already engaged in building the future around us through the creation of a forgiven and redeemed society, a community in which old wrongs become an opportunity to create new life, in which the old, double humanity of people opposed to one another is replaced by the new, single humanity of Christ's peace.

We have been saying all along that forgiveness, like repentance, is a form of conversion, of getting a new mind. This mind— the mind of forgiveness and peace, the mind of the age to come— is the mind we were talking about. This is the vision in God's mind that we are invited to catch and share: a humanity genuinely at peace, not under compulsion or out of duty, but because we have all come to share a new vision of love as forgiveness and so to participate in God's joy.

Love, Not Duty

It's important to keep forgiveness in this context. Forgiveness derives from God's life flowing into us through the Spirit and leading us to grow and mature in God's love. If we let ourselves go back to thinking of forgiveness merely in terms of rules and duty, we've missed the boat. We want to forgive, we need to forgive, and we can forgive—not because we ought to, but because forgiveness is a source of life and joy for us and an expression of life in us.

I don't mean that forgiveness is therefore easy. It's not. In some ways, it might actually seem easier if it *were* just a duty and not a matter of personal transformation. If you can think of forgiveness as a duty, then your only problem is how to convince yourself that you've done it. No personal transformation is required. It becomes a matter of just checking things off your "to do" list. As long as you can conceal your continuing animosity and ill will from yourself as well as your neighbors, then, as far as you know, you've done your duty. End of story.

Real forgiveness is more complex and involves a lot more of ourselves. And it's always, to a significant degree, a gift from God rather than something we do on our own. I've already suggested some ways to cultivate a certain openness to it. Now we can think more about what happens as we open up to forgiveness. How does this occur in our lives?

Above all, it is a process, not a simple event. In many cases, we don't forgive easily; and those, of course, are the cases that most concern us. When forgiveness does come easily for us, we probably don't have a lot of questions about it. But when it doesn't, we find ourselves asking how this process works and how we can cooperate with it more readily. The key, I believe, lies in the recognition that forgiveness is primarily oriented toward the future.

Forgiveness begins, of course, in the midst of tension. When we confront the negative realities of our situation with attention to truth, we find ourselves in confusion and disarray. The past and present have become problematic. We know that we've been wronged. Our lives have been disrupted, physically, emotionally, or spiritually—or often all three. Sometimes we even find ourselves in a double relationship with the person who has harmed us. It may be someone we have respected, loved, counted as a friend. We may feel both continuing affection and anger, helplessness, and other emotions we'd rather avoid.

We know that we cannot stand to remain permanently in this divided and disturbed state. We don't want the future to be merely an extension of the past and present. But how do we create new possibilities? And what keeps us from moving forward? One thing that holds us back is the fact that the future is scary. It contains much that is unknown, and it is largely out of our control.

The future is not absolutely out of our control, of course; there's a certain amount we can do to affect it. But our influence on it always has limits, and we don't even know exactly where those limits are. We learn them largely by running up against them. The future always brings with it the possibility of surprise. Actually, it's more than a possibility; it's a near certainty.

The Promise of a Future Out of Our Control

The gospel does something quite daring with this uncontrolled, unpredictable, threatening, surprising aspect of the future. It takes the very thing that alarms us and turns it into a promise. It tells us that the other name for surprise is grace. It claims that, even in our most uncertain and difficult moments, the great animating principle behind all that exists is not fate or chance or suffering or illusion, but love acting through forgiveness.

What was at the center of Jesus' message? Good news! Gospel! If it's news, it's a surprise; but the surprise turns out to be good. And the surprise is this: You aren't on trial, after all. God deals with us not according to our earned credits (in which case the only surprises would come from having done a sloppy job of our own moral bookkeeping) but according to grace, according to the gift of free forgiveness. As we begin to accept that—and it isn't the easiest or most obvious thing in the world, though it is the deepest of all truths—we also begin to accept the unpredictability of the future as promise rather than threat. We feel less and less need to control the working out of forgiveness and its effects. We leave more in the hands of God and see ourselves simply as participating in God's great work of redemption and renewal.

We can't even retain the right to put our own private spin on the future. We might like to build a self-serving future based on our private set of plans, giving fine accommodations to our friends and assigning a small but decent garret to our old enemy. (We are religious folk, after all, and not too inclined to bear a grudge.) But it won't work that way. The future is always a result of gift *and response*. Yet, the fact that we don't have "complete creative control" may actually be liberating. We can afford to let the future emerge as it must—from the interaction between us and those who have harmed us, and the grace of God.

Forgiveness doesn't pretend to be in complete control of the future. It doesn't need to be. It has the nerve to do its part and to leave the rest in the hands of God—and of the ones we have forgiven. For the other persons involved will always have something to contribute unless they refuse completely (more on this later). If they do refuse, that won't prevent the future from taking shape in a meaningful way; but if they cooperate, their contribution will help shape what emerges.

The Greek word that we translate as "forgive" (*aphiemi*) means basically "to let go." "Forgive us our debts" means "Let our debts go; turn them loose." Forgiveness involves a letting go—letting go our investment in the past so that we can turn toward the future; letting go our need to control the other; even letting go our sense of our own righteousness so that something new can happen in the world. Forgiveness builds the future. It does so not by controlling the future but by letting go of the hostility that the past has engendered.

Forgiveness, then, is always a daring and risky act. It might be impossible, if we hadn't discovered that it's God's way of inviting us into God's own life. Forgiveness is the mind of God, the life of God. The gain of sharing in that life outweighs the risk, because it brings us into God's joy.

The Heart of Forgiveness

Forgiveness, then, looks to the future. Yet it doesn't claim to control the future in detail. But if we're not expecting to control our enemies by forgiving them and if we're not trying to build a future purely to our own liking, what *are* we doing when we forgive? We're doing two things: (1) we're admitting that we still belong to the same human family as our enemies, and (2) we're leaving the door open to the hope of a shared future. What does this mean?

We forgive one another by acknowledging that *we're all in this together*, whether we like it or not. No matter how evil my neighbor may have become, this person is still a human being. This person is not beyond God's love. Perhaps at some point the evil person will wake up to that love and be both shamed by it and drawn toward it. Perhaps this person will discover something of the mind of God and accept it and experience new life. Perhaps this person will surrender to the God who went on loving anyway. Perhaps it will be someone like John Newton, the man who wrote "Amazing Grace," who went from being a slave trader to being an advocate of love and grace for all.

By saying that we're all in this together, I don't mean to suggest a kind of moral relativism that says everybody is equally bad (or good). I can't see any evidence for that. The world would be better off with more evidence of human responsibility and civility and basic decency, more integrity and restraint on the part of campaigning politicians, more openness and generosity on the part of churches, more respect for God's creation, more care and concern for children—you can add your own items to the list and we might very likely agree on most of them. When we find ourselves dealing with decent, responsible people, all of life is given a new hope and delight.

The point isn't to pretend that everybody's already on the same moral level, the point is that not one of us can escape being human. Within our human limits, not one of us is yet perfected. Different as we are from one another, vast as the gap is between the most saintly of saints and the most vicious of genocidal demagogues, we are still more like one another than we are like anyone or anything else in the universe. And our most fundamental likeness is our ongoing ability to change and to grow and to respond to love.

We're so far from being perfect at this point in our experience that we can't even be too sure what perfection would look like. Sometimes, as we've said, we imagine it in terms that are so fixed and unchanging as to be really inhuman. We think of perfection as never doing anything wrong. (For most of us, I imagine it's a bit late to make that one work.) Or we think of it as being absolutely and fully vindicated, so that the whole world can see that we deserved much better than we got. Or perhaps we think of it as doing a perfect job of repentance. At the very least, we imagine it as being better than the people around us. ("Oh Lord, I may not be much, but just look at those other people...")

But the best vision we have of human perfection is of a very different order. It's the risen Jesus sharing bread with a group of bewildered disciples, offering his hands and feet to them to inspect and see the evidence of his self-giving, calling them by name, welcoming them back to his love even after they have abandoned him, holding a family reunion where all are welcome. Now there's a vision of human perfection! And it's not about being right or about being vindicated, it's about love.

So we forgive one another—and ask God to forgive us in the same measure—because we're all in this together. Our forgiveness of one another is a proclamation of our human unity, the unity that the author of Ephesians wrote about, the unity that Jesus created on the cross. The best human hope is to grow toward the loving and giving maturity that we see in Jesus. As we grow toward that maturity, the more loving we will become and the less we'll want to leave anybody behind. We're all in it together. That's forgiveness.

The other side to forgiveness is *keeping the door open* to some kind of shared future. When you hold that door open, you can't guarantee that the person who harmed you will ever walk through it with you. We can't control that. And if we could, it wouldn't be a free choice, and it wouldn't have much meaning. Even God doesn't force anyone to choose the good.

God leaves us free to stay outside the circle of love. The beautiful thing about the gospel is that God's love for us never ceases. The scary thing about it is that we're free to ignore that fact forever. We're all free to go off and build our own hells and inhabit them. The gate to heaven can stand open forever, but that doesn't guarantee that everyone will go in. Probably most of us can sense within ourselves a little something that could conceivably choose to be miserable in a world of our own making rather than to be blissfully happy in God's family.

So we can't force those we forgive to go through the door with us, but we can keep it open. And onto what does the door open? In broad terms, it opens onto the world of peace and joy and reunion, the world of Jesus' resurrection. As to the details of that world, those remain to be seen. Not even God has predetermined them. The open door reveals a possibility: What might we build together? That's the landscape it opens on. The building that will rise to grace that terrain is still waiting to be thought and lived into being. It won't be a brand-new building, erected on some flat space bulldozed out of the hillside. It will take account of the site as the past has shaped it. There may be some wreckage there from previous buildings destroyed or damaged by the wrong that was done. Some of the old buildings may be solid enough to be reha- bilitated. Some will have to be cleared away. Some of the debris may turn out to be useful in the new construction.

But this future that we glimpse through the door held open in forgiveness—this future will have to be built on the spot. No truly human future is prefabricated. This is no suburban devel- opment with a choice of four floor plans and six facades. It's all owner-designed and -built with the help of whatever good advice you have at hand. You won't know for sure what it will be like until you are moving in.

Acknowledging our common humanity, offering to build a future together—that's what forgiveness is. It's something of a voyage into the unknown. And, yes, there's an unavoidable ele- ment of risk in it. The future is not in our control. It will emerge in the process of forgiveness itself. We trust the process only because we see that God is behind it, moving in mysterious ways to create the surprises of grace.

Risk, Not Stupidity

So forgiveness always involves risk, but taking a risk is not the same thing as going soft in the head. Jumping across an alarming but nonetheless jumpable chasm to save your life is one thing; leaping off a cliff for no reason at all is another. Forgiving those who sin against us isn't a purposeless activity. We have a goal in mind. We know we can't control the results exactly. But we do have a purpose in forgiving, and we need to be attentive to that purpose, to be alert in forwarding it.

Consider the story of Joseph (Gen. 37, 39–45). He and his brothers did one another some serious wrongs, and those wrongs came back to haunt them. And Joseph, who had been most deeply harmed, turned out to hold the key to the future.

Now, Joseph was not the nicest sibling you could hope to have. He was his father's pet. He got better clothes than his brothers, and he wore them all the time. He got to stay at home and keep his hands clean and eat well while his brothers were out sweating in the pastures. He had dreams in which he was the center of the world and all his family had to pay him reverence—and he had the bad grace to tell everybody about the dreams. It's hard to feel a lot of sympathy for him. But he didn't deserve to be seized by his brothers, roughed up, dumped down a well, and sold into slavery in a distant land.

Joseph's brothers carried the guilt of their actions with them the rest of their lives. They were pretty successful at hiding their deed. They splattered Joseph's fancy coat with blood so that their father would think that he was dead, and the family went on without him. But they carried the wrong inside themselves.

You remember how the story goes: Joseph rises, against all odds, to become the most powerful person in Egypt. He is in charge of all the resources of the kingdom during a time of terrible famine. The same famine affects Canaan, too, and forces his brothers to come to Egypt to buy grain. There they are told they'll have to see this powerful man who is in charge of everything. They don't recognize Joseph in his Egyptian clothes (even finer than what their father had given him long before), but he recognizes them. When he discovers that they still feel guilt over what they did to him, he is overcome with emotion.

And then he sets them up. He deals strictly but decently with them, and he sets up a situation in which they have to repeat the decision of earlier years. His little brother Benjamin is now their father's pet. What will the other brothers do with *him*? Will they sacrifice him the way they did Joseph? No, when push comes to shove, they prove to have changed. They walk through the door Joseph has opened for them, even though they don't in fact understand who has opened it. They decide to salvage what they can of the mutual responsibility of brothers, and their leader, Judah, ancestor of Jesus, asks to suffer Benjamin's punishment in his place so that their father can have his youngest son back.

At that point, we are told, Joseph could no longer control his emotions. He made his Egyptian retainers leave and, alone, he revealed his true identity to his brothers so that he, too, could walk through the door of forgiveness with them into whatever future they would shape together.

Did Joseph take risks here? Most certainly. However grand his state, he was emotionally vulnerable from the moment his brothers appeared before him in Egypt. Yet his hurt and anger didn't dictate his actions. He had the patience to find out who and what they were ready to become. He didn't take refuge in his own righteousness or his own victimhood. He stayed open to the future.

Joseph could do all this because he was already in the process of forgiving his brothers. His soul was no longer imprisoned by the wrong they had done him. He didn't need revenge. He didn't feel an obligation to make nice. He didn't try to pretend anything away. He accepted that they were still human beings like him, and he was prepared to see who they were becoming and what future they could build together.

What Joseph did may seem like rather a hardheaded kind of forgiveness, but there's nothing wrong with that. It was completely genuine, and it opened the door to a shared future. That's all that's important. And it wasn't just Joseph's head that was involved, but his whole self. It was a triumph of love.

But Is This Enough?

Someone may be thinking, "Yes, but doesn't Jesus set up a higher standard? Turning the other cheek. Going the extra mile. Ultimately, suffering martyrdom. Isn't that quite a different matter from this very practical approach to forgiveness?" Well, actually, no.

Jesus does tell us to turn the other cheek. But turning the other cheek doesn't mean complete passivity. It means that we are not in a hurry to judge, that we give others the benefit of the doubt at first. It is a kind of test: Did you really mean that slap, or was it an act of passion that bypassed your mind and heart? Will you do it again, once it's been called to your attention? Turning the other cheek is a question addressed to the wrongdoer.

Joseph is a good example of exactly this. He had the power simply to punish his brothers, but he didn't. He put them to a test, but he was perfectly willing for them to pass it. His real interest was to find out who they had become and what they were prepared to do to avoid repeating their old offense. The test to which he subjected them was really an open door into the future, though they could not tell that at the time.

And going the extra mile isn't a matter of obsequious acquiescence. It's an ironic reassertion of one's own independence. In Jesus' day, it appears that a Roman soldier had the right to demand just one mile of portage service from the local Jewish civilian. If a person went two miles, the second mile could only be a gift, and that, of course, changes the relationship altogether. Giving a gift asserts equality, at the very least, between the giver and the receiver.

The same is true of forgiveness. From Proverbs onward, biblical writers have reminded us that forgiveness can be a way of heaping coals on the heads of those who have wronged us (Prov. 25:22; Rom. 12:20). You assume a kind of power when you harm me. I assume another and more inclusive kind of power when I consent to forgive you. Forgiveness can be a way of leveling the playing field, of claiming full equality with or even superiority to the person who wronged me.

But what about martyrdom? Isn't suffering something to be prized by Christians? Isn't it always better to suffer rather than to resist or to demand something from those who have harmed us, as Joseph did? No. Christian faith, even if there have been some peculiarly masochistic misinterpretations of it, has no love affair with suffering.

We forget that the term *martyr* doesn't really mean "sufferer." That's the way we use it carelessly in our everyday language, but it really means "witness." Jesus didn't suffer because he wanted to or because he couldn't help it. He suffered because he deliberately provoked the religious authorities to show their true selves. He succeeded. He forced them to reveal the truth about themselves, about their self-serving and limited conception of their holy task. In the process, he died. But in dying, he witnessed to God's love and forgiveness even for those who killed him. For our sakes, he would not compromise that ultimate truth.

When suffering is the only possible means of witnessing effectively, we accept it as Christians. By the grace of God, it has proved very powerful over the ages. But for most of us most of the time, the best way to witness to the truth is not by suffering but by standing up, holding up your head, telling what really happened, making a fuss, leaving an abusive situation, calling for justice.

In Luke's Gospel, Jesus tells a parable about a woman who was an authentic martyr. She was a widow, putting her at a grave disadvantage in the legal system of Jesus' day, which took only men seriously. As a widow, she had to fend for herself, and that was almost a legal impossibility. Worse yet, this widow had to depend for justice on a judge who, Jesus tells us, "neither feared God nor respected humanity." What did the widow do? Did she retire passively from the fray and concentrate on forgiving the immoral judge? No, she badgered him ceaselessly, until finally he said, "Even though I don't fear God and have no respect for humanity, just because this widow is a nuisance, I'll take care of her case before she finally wears me out by coming to badger me." Quite right, says Jesus; this kind of witnessing works (Luke 18:1–8).

Yes, Christian faith does have a commitment to martyrdom,

but to martyrdom in its true meaning as "witnessing," witnessing above all to God's love and truth. Martyrdom does not mean living like a doormat. There is nothing in Jesus' behavior or teaching that encourages a life of complete passivity, a life that invites people to step on us. The life of forgiveness would be a strange and harmful kindness if it meant encouraging people in actions that are good neither for them nor for the people they harm.

Forgiveness acknowledges our common humanity and holds open a door to the future. But it also calls things by their true names. It isn't timid but fearless. It's neither mealymouthed nor abusive, but straightforward. It doesn't seek to harm others by telling the truth, but neither does it refrain from telling the truth just because someone might be inconvenienced or their wrongs brought to light. Forgiveness assumes a bold and engaged way of living.

Forgiveness, after all, isn't a retreat from reality. To the contrary, it always looks outward. It is the most generous of loves. It is God's best gift to us. We accept it for ourselves. We extend it to one another. It turns out to be far more than at first it seemed. It is the spiritual river of life that carries the past along, washing it clean of its wrongs, into the as-yet-uncertain future—a future that will culminate in the age to come. By forgiving and being forgiven, we bring that life, our true citizenship, with us into the midst of this world, and we bring this world one step closer to its own future fulfillment.

God forgives all alike. As we learn forgiveness, we find ourselves participating in the very life of God and therefore living with the kind of boldness that befits children of God's own household.

Some Practical Problems

❦

U p to this point, I've been treating forgiveness in fairly general terms, but there are also some particular circumstances and situations that can make it particularly difficult for us to forgive. I want to examine a few of those and offer some reflections on why they're difficult and what steps we can take to meet them. I am thinking, in this chapter, particularly of problems that arise from the behavior of other people—often from the specific character of wrongs done to us. There are no simple, direct, infallible solutions to these problems; yet we are not helpless before them, either.

The difficulties in question here arise out of the nature of the wrong done to us, or out of the attitude adopted by the one who committed the wrong, or out of the ongoing relationship we have with that person. These are circumstances largely outside our control, and they may make forgiveness particularly difficult for us to give because it doesn't seem to lead to any healthy result. At times, indeed, forgiveness may seem almost to acquiesce in the wrong or to give it approval—things we rightly shrink from doing. Yet, we still have the need, in these situations, to turn old wrongs loose, if only for our own peace and freedom.

Apologies—and Their Absence

We all know that when we have done someone harm, we have the power to help heal the hurt by offering an apology and, where

73

appropriate, making restitution. Jesus tells us not only to forgive those who have wronged us but also to ask for forgiveness when we have wronged another: "If you are offering your gift at the altar and there you remember that your brother or sister has anything against you, leave your gift there before the altar and go, first be reconciled to your sister or brother and then come and offer your gift" (Matt. 5:23–24).

This is partly just good practical sense. As the author of Proverbs reminds us, "A soft answer turneth away wrath" (Prov. 15:1 AV). But it's more than just good policy. By offering an expression of sorrow and regret, we can make it simpler for those we have wronged to move beyond the hurtful past. We simplify their process of dealing with the harm. How? By confirming their understanding of what happened and by acknowledging that they have power to help heal the relationship. The apology turns out to be a kind of gift to the one we have offended and, in the limited way possible for us when we're in the wrong, a contribution to the shared process of forgiveness and reconciliation.

A good apology, one that will actually contribute to this process, requires tact and respect. It must be a gift. I can offer it, but I cannot insist that it be accepted. As the wrongdoer, I have no right to *demand* forgiveness; that would only be imposing yet another burden on the person I have wronged. In any case, forgiveness comes as a gift or not at all. The apology does not *compel* forgiveness or *earn* it or *purchase* it; it only seeks to smooth the way and make it easier for the offended party to give the gift of forgiveness in return.

To this end, an apology should usually be a plain and simple admission of fault without a catalog of extenuating circumstances or self-defense. We are asking the offended party not to feel sorry for us or to excuse us but to forgive us for something we are sorry we have done. We are sorry both that we have harmed another and that we have broken a relationship thereby.

This rules out clever casuistries—for example, the kind of apology that begins, "I'm sorry that what I did upset you," implying that there was nothing really wrong about it and that your reaction was probably excessive. Such verbal sleights try to create the appearance of an apology without actually apologizing. They are of no value spiritually. For the wronged party, they only add insult to injury. For the wrongdoer, they are spiritually dangerous, because they are really a form of hypocrisy.

The spiritual value of an apology is, first, that it is an occasion to evaluate ourselves accurately, with "neither fear nor favor." Spiritual guides have always advocated self-examination as a means to self-knowledge. And self-knowledge is necessary if we are to become intimate with God. How can we participate in any intimate relationship without having some initial notion (hopefully, a growing notion) of who we are? The point of self-examination, then, and of the confession to which it leads, is not to grovel but to know oneself and to present oneself fairly and accurately, including the things we may be ashamed of.

The faith of the gospel makes it possible to do this with a steadier vision, because we know that God's love for us is not dependent on our being perfect. If we imagine that our standing with God is dependent on our doing everything right, we are deeply tempted to cover up our faults. We become masters of disguise. We create a facade of exceptional virtue in one part of our lives to compensate for the vices of another. We may even make a show of confessing one set of faults to keep ourselves from looking at another set that disturbs us more. A favorite technique of religious charlatans is to focus on sexual faults, which most people in our culture feel anxious about, to distract their followers from noticing more grievous sins such as greed, hypocrisy, and hostility toward other people. An honest apology is a fine spiritual discipline for cutting through such nonsense.

Second, the making of an apology is a way of participating in God's gracious and generous project of redeeming the world through the spread of forgiveness. Our apology puts us "in the way" of forgiveness. It is the one contribution we can make when we have wronged another. I do not mean that our repentance *earns* forgiveness, either from God or from the injured party. As I have already said, true forgiveness is possible only as gift, never as payment.

In relation to God, there is no need to earn forgiveness, because, as Paul said, God extended the offer of forgiveness long before we were ready to take advantage of it. What repentance does is accept the gift and make use of it. In the case of those whom we have wronged, our apology makes their path to forgiveness easier and prepares us to receive the gift if it is given. By acknowledging our failure, we affirm that the offended party has power either to forgive or to deny forgiveness; we confess that person's power in our relationship, admitting that we are now dependent on him or her for restoration.

When no apology or acknowledgment of wrongdoing is forthcoming, it can make the work of the forgiver more difficult—but not impossible. What are you to do when you are the offended party and the offender walks away as though nothing has happened or as if the actions were perfectly justified? This is a serious dilemma. People may feel paralyzed in the process of forgiveness and therefore trapped by the old wrong, unable to leave it behind and move on without the cooperation of the other person.

It may even seem like a mistake to forgive the unrepentant. Won't such forgiveness just encourage the same behavior again? Isn't it an absurd act of acquiescence in our own suffering? It's all well and good to say that God forgives us before we repent, but we human beings, unlike God, are not infinite—in life, in love, in patience, in riches. We can indeed imitate God's love, but there is no piety in pretending that we, too, have infinite resources. Isn't it better to admit that we have to place some limits on forgiveness? Isn't it better to leave the unrepentant entirely to God's forgiveness?

The answer is "no," but it has more to do with our own spiritual lives and our own relationship with God than with the wrongdoer who refuses to apologize. Forgiveness, as I have been saying, is primarily not about the past but about the future. There is a strange sense in which forgiveness isn't primarily about the wrong being forgiven or about the person who did it—despite the fact that they are both grammatical objects of the verb *forgive*! Forgiveness is about the forgiver.

Forgiveness is about who we—the people forgiving—are and

who we are becoming. It's about turning loose of the past so that we can live fully in the present while we build a new and surprising future with God and with one another. Although the other person's apology would help us in concluding the old chapter and moving on, we can do that anyway, with God's help, through the discovery of new riches in our own lives. We are, after all, falling ever more deeply into love with God—the love that God is sharing with all the world. As we forgive, we discover our new wealth. As we discover our new wealth, we find it easier to share by forgiving.

In the process, we wind up incidentally keeping a door open for future reconciliation and rebuilding. Think about the Joseph story again. Joseph certainly didn't get an apology from his brothers. Yet he somehow turned loose of his (perfectly justified) anger and resentment toward them. Of course, he was caught up in new struggles and opportunities. Before he knew it, he was enduring slavery in Egypt. Then he was trying to fend off, in a politic way, the dangerous overtures of Potiphar's wife. Then he was suffering through another undeserved spell in prison. Then, after all these struggles, he suddenly had the daunting responsibility of seeing Egypt through a major natural disaster.

Joseph was busy dealing with a full life. And that is at least partly the point, isn't it? He lived in the present, working with what he had been given, building a worthwhile future. He hung onto his sense of God's love—his sense that God had some goodwill, even some plan, for him. He remembered his brothers' treachery, but it didn't dominate his existence. Eventually, he was able to say to his brothers, "It was God who did this, not you"— God did it for the sake of the blessing that Joseph would eventually bring about through his improbable history. Joseph wasn't making nice with his brothers when he said this, or sparing their feelings. He was telling them what his life had come to mean to him. It was dominated not by past wrongs but by a sense of the richness of life lived in friendship with God.

When the offender doesn't repent and apologize, then, what do we do? Perhaps at first we are caught in a tangle of emotions.

We are hurt, angry, resentful and stymied in our efforts to escape these unpleasant feelings. We would like to have the one who harmed us acknowledge the truth of the past with an apology. We would like to see signs of repentance that might make some new and life-giving relationship possible. All this is reasonable. It would be helpful. But it isn't necessary.

God's forgiveness flows out of the richness of God's own life and seeks to share that richness with others. It isn't an end in itself but a means to draw us all toward a similar richness of life. Forgiveness releases us from bondage to the past precisely so that we can live in and by the riches of God's love. We can participate in this same generous life as God's friends. We can get on with building and enjoying this life. The more we share in it and take delight in it, the more readily we can forgive.

There's an analogy with something Paul says about marriage. This was a subject on which Paul was quite definite and even rather rule-bound (despite his general suspicion of legally based goodness), yet he was prepared to acknowledge that some circumstances cannot be mended. In the case of the believer who is rejected by a nonbelieving spouse, he says, "Let the person go. The brother or sister is not enslaved in such situations. But God has called you in peace" (1 Cor. 7:15).

When the wrongdoer will not cooperate in a process of reconciliation, let the person go. Let others find the path, with God's help, that will lead them to new life. Your own path is peace. You are not enslaved to the past; God has called you in peace. God has called you to life. Look about you for the signs and opportunities of that life—and live it.

If, like Joseph, we seek the good that is possible in our present situation, we need not be enslaved by the pain of past wrongs or held back by the wrongdoer's refusal to repent or to apologize. Forgiveness is a gift that turns out to benefit the giver even more than the receiver, since it frees us of having to be slaves to the past. It is a direct expression of the increasing richness of our lives with God.

And so we forgive people anyway. We forgive even without help from the offender. We do it for our own sake, so that we can get on with our God-given lives. And if, at some point, things change and the offender does want to go through the door we've kept open, we can follow Joseph's lead. If we haven't been living with bated breath, waiting for that moment, we won't refuse it, either.

The Absent Offender

Sometimes the person who has wronged us doesn't just fail to apologize but disappears completely. Perhaps the wrong was some random act of violence or theft, and we never knew who perpetrated it. Or it may be that a family member or friend or associate at work harms us and then moves away and breaks all contact. Perhaps the person who wronged us is even dead and, it would seem, conclusively out of reach.

This situation may be particularly difficult for those who were wronged as children and have carried the consequences with them ever since. Often we wake up only much later in our lives to the extent and meaning of what was done to us as children. Even after we have recognized it as wrong, it may be a long time before we feel sufficiently secure in our adult identity to challenge the offender. By that time, it may be too late to deal with that person directly. That leaves us with a strong sense of unfinished business, which can be very painful to us. Having spent years wrestling with this long-buried wrong and preparing to handle it consciously and responsibly as an adult, how is a person to deal with the fact that there is no possibility of "closure" with the person or persons responsible?

Here we need to distinguish between two things that are often intertwined in our daily lives: forgiveness and reconciliation. They are related. Ideally, we like them to go together. But they are not the same thing. Reconciliation takes at least two people, but forgiveness can happen unilaterally—indeed, that is its normal form. By forgiveness, I let the offense and the offender go. I allow that reality to recede into the past while I get on with my own life.

In the process, the past loses its power to keep me from living here and now. I don't mean that we are ever entirely free of the past. In fact, we are always shaped by it. But that shaping can take many different forms—some harmful, some helpful. Just as Joseph took a past that was full of disasters and came to see it as a means by which God had shaped him for blessing, we, too, can find even the evils of our past turning into building materials for the present and the future. We do this when we claim the divine grace, freely given, to recognize the past harm and to let it go (without in any way denying its reality or its seriousness), and so to continue growing in love.

The absence of the wrongdoer, then, complicates forgiveness, but it doesn't make forgiveness impossible. But what about reconciliation? In cases such as these, it may seem pointless to speak of building any kind of future with a person who is at best absent and at worst may be totally unknown to us. Does forgiveness mean simply writing these people off?

In the immediate moment, that may in fact be the case: "The brother or sister is not enslaved in such situations. But God has called you in peace." That, in itself, is a gain. You are free to pursue peace, with the help of God, unhindered by the absence of the offender. But the gospel is not just about the inner peace of individuals. God loves every individual—and all the world. Christian faith, when it is working, tends to lead us toward a big picture of the world and God's activity in it.

As we cultivate the power of forgiving and even the habit of forgiving, we are in fact creating a new world around us, one that is slowly beginning to reflect more and more of the life of the age to come. As we do so, we are creating a world in which love, forgiveness, and reconciliation triumph, in which we are united with one another in the assurance of God's goodwill toward us. As we absorb more and more of God's generous love into our lives, we give the world around us a reason and an opportunity to change.

I'm not suggesting magical solutions. The world as we know it is very resistant to love. It isn't going to surrender easily. For that matter, even those of us who have been touched by God's love and brought to faith and new life by it seldom surrender easily! But love is the only power that can heal and renew and bring about reconciliation. Through our forgiveness of one another, even of the absent offender, love makes its way through the world.

When I am teaching, I often feel that I am repaying a debt in an odd sort of way. What I owe to my own teachers I repay by giving to my students. In this process the world is enriched in ways that direct exchanges between two parties could never achieve alone. I think that if we cultivate the gift of forgiveness, even where it cannot affect the relationship between us and those who have actually wronged us, its effects will still spill over onto the world at large. If reconciliation cannot reunite me with the one who wronged me, it can still work at reuniting the broken communities where we live here and now.

Moreover, we Christians are people of the resurrection. The good news that has brought us new life here and now, we believe, will reach its consummation in the life of the age to come. God has many surprises up God's sleeve yet. It would be a mistake to assume dogmatically that reconciliation with those who have wronged us and then run away out of our lives is eternally impossible.

In the age to come, there is nothing to fear. No one will be free to be abusive there. But it is not a static world. If it's truly a world for human beings, it will continue to be a place of growth and learning and change. We are, even now, only in the early stages of this, our true life. God forces no one to enter the life of that age, but all are welcome. If we do choose to enter, it is because we have caught some glimmer of its great beauty and delight. We are drawn to it by a deep desire, even though we know that to take part in it, we shall have to become, in some degree and in unforeseen ways, new people.

Perhaps those who have wronged us will choose not to enter that world. When we wrong one another, it is often out of a desire to exert control over our lives, to make things be exactly as we want them. Perhaps the age to come, with its risk of becoming new, will be too terrifying for that reason. Perhaps we shall never again meet those who have wronged us. Yet I have at least a hope that it won't be so, a hope that no human being is capable of eternally rejecting the beauty and wonder of our true life. I think we are at least capable of being converted by it. We can still hope—as God, too, hopes—that all will be part of the great multitude that repents (in William Temple's sense of the word) and takes up the work of forgiveness and enters into the joy of God's family, at last reassembled in our true home.

Whether such future reconciliation happens for us or not, I believe that our forgiving of those who have harmed us is a gift to ourselves and to the rest of the world. By putting aside our obsession with the past, our imprisonment in its wrongs, we become free people again, no longer enslaved, ready to participate in the present and the future. Our past can become part of our future in the form of a blessing instead of a curse. The richer life that we then enjoy spills over onto those around us as we become agents of the reconciliation of all things. Forgiveness of the absent is not easy, but it turns out to be both a good thing in itself and a source of other good as well.

The Abusive Situation and the Repeat Offender

Another class of problems are those where harm has become habitual. Here, the one who wrongs us is not absent but all too present. It's one thing to forgive individual wrongs done to you. In such cases, it seems possible to leave the wrongs in the past and move on to reconciliation. It's quite another thing to forgive when you have every reason to think that the wrongdoer will continue to commit the same offense over and over again in the future.

In some cases, the two situations may be hard to distinguish at first. The doer of the harm may be overcome with regret, may apologize and promise not to do the same thing again—and then may prove unable or unwilling actually to fulfill these undertakings. At the first occurrence, forgiveness seems relatively easy. But at the third or fifth or seventeenth repetition, one begins to realize that something is seriously awry. At this point, you have encountered not just a single harmful act but a destructive habit or perspective or social structure that must be resisted.

One classic example is the case of battered spouses or life partners. What does forgiveness mean in a situation where someone very close to you—someone you love—has repeatedly abused you, whether physically or emotionally? Do you work to forgive each individual incident—and wait meekly for it to happen again? Is that what marriage demands? Is that what God's love demands?

No. At some point, we have to see that it is no longer a case of isolated incidents. The situation itself has become the offense. Remember that forgiveness always begins with honesty. It begins with trying to understand exactly what the offense has been and to confront it in all its dimensions. The process of forgiveness can't even get started until we do that.

How does a battered spouse or partner enter on the path of forgiveness? Not by pointlessly enduring one assault after another. The first step is to say, "I'm being abused by this person who claims to love me, and this is wrong." You may have analyzed the situation inadequately before. You may have been saying, "I've been battered once or twice, but I don't think it'll happen again." But at some point, you begin to realize that this isn't a matter of individual events to be forgiven individually, it is an ongoing offense that has to be dealt with in some quite different way.

So the first thing is to admit the truth. And the next thing is to get out of that situation. Forgiveness doesn't consist of soft-headedness. It is not a way of denying, ignoring, condoning, or tolerating wrong. It begins by recognizing and naming the wrongdoing and, if at all possible, bringing it to a halt.

Abused partners are often reluctant to take this step. They have loved the persons who are now abusing them. The abusers often claim to love them and may show signs of regret after instances of abuse. There is an ongoing hope that the victim's love can transform the abusive partner. Perhaps the abused partner even hopes that the simple act of forgiving the other will restore the relationship. So great is our longing for the warmth of feeling and the security that we associate with family life that we find it relatively easy to delude ourselves.

After single incidents of wrongdoing between people who have had a strong relationship, there can sometimes be a fairly easy reconciliation and restoration. But habitual patterns will not normally yield to such immediate solutions. They run too deep. In cases of abuse toward spouses and partners, they tend to reflect deep-seated problems that the offenders may be reluctant to explore or to change. In such cases, an effort to move directly, by way of forgiveness, from the individual harmful act back to the warmth of familial and sexual affection is normally doomed to failure.

Forgiveness, here, needs to respond to the whole pattern, and we need to distinguish clearly between the two distinct processes of forgiveness and reconciliation. Forgiveness can hold open the possibility of reconciliation. But it will say, "If there's going to be a future between the two of us, it has to be a nonabusive one." No other kind of relationship is appropriate for those who are citizens of the age to come. No other kind of relationship can endure in that age where harm ceases to be a possibility. The only forgiving and loving thing here is to demand change.

This principle holds true not only for individuals and couples but also for larger social groups where abuse has become habitual. Abusive assumptions can sometimes become part of the accepted norms of social interaction. Racism, for example, is simply the assumption that wrongs done to people of a particular skin color don't "count." People can live entire lives in a racist society without really noticing that this constitutes a kind of habitual abuse of others—provided, of course, that they are on the giving rather than the receiving end of the abuse.

Racism can't be forgiven before it is named and resisted. And naming it is not simply a matter of accumulating a catalog of individual offenses. It means calling the whole system to account, including the presuppositions behind it that encourage people of one color routinely to abuse people of another color. If we try to deal with issues of racism on the basis of one

incident at a time, we will be missing most of what is so power-
fully wrong with it.

Forgiving racism, then, doesn't mean ignoring it or tolerating
it. The process of forgiveness begins only when we recognize it,
confront it wherever and whenever possible, and insist that something better is possible in our future. The same holds true with all
kinds of structural social abuses. It is true of sexism, with its habit
of treating the humanity of women as deficient, and of hetero-
sexism, with its similar treatment of sexual minorities. It is true of
anti-Semitism and of all other religious and ethnic prejudices—all
the habits of thought and action by which one group denies the
full humanity of another.

Forgiveness is not an alternative to political action in these
cases; it's actually one foundation for them. Perhaps, in the long
run, it's the healthiest foundation. Political action by the
oppressed often begins in anger. Perhaps anger is the only emotion sharp enough to prompt most people into action in oppressive circumstances. But for political action to keep going, it must
also be built on a hope that something better can be created. And
to create that better society, one must find a vision that can
include one's opponents—a future that will accommodate both
us and our oppressors in a new and more equitable public order.
Only forgiveness can free us to imagine such a future.

But it may, of course, happen that a person finds herself or
himself in a situation where neither escape nor political con-
frontation is possible. What about the situation of a slave, for
example, in the antebellum South? What about the situation of a
Christian martyr during the late Roman Empire, or someone
caught up in the Holocaust, or a prisoner of conscience under any
of the twentieth century's many totalitarian regimes? What about
a battered wife in a culture that recognizes no real rights for
women? These are the extreme examples—the most difficult situations for forgiveness that I can imagine.

I admit that, here, I am in no position to give advice. The
astonishing thing to me is that even in such situations, people
have sometimes found ways to retain their dignity as human

beings. Like Jesus before the authorities, some people have found the power to stand up straight and meet their attackers head-on with grace. They have not allowed their oppressors' arrogance to deprive them of their sense of worth.

Such persons have found the power to live and die without hate. They have been able to recognize both their own humanity and that of their jailers and oppressors. They have discovered the divine power of love and forgiveness moving through their lives in such a way as to be able to extend that love and forgiveness, without denying the evil of their situation or surrendering to it, to their persecutors.

Such persons have fulfilled, intentionally or not, the advice Jesus gives his disciples in Luke's Gospel about living in times of great danger and challenge. When the signs of the last days begin to happen, he says, "Stand up straight and hold your heads up, because your redemption is near" (21:28). This is the posture in which to meet catastrophe and cataclysm and apparent defeat. It neither shrinks from an expected blow nor coils itself to return it. It is simply and purely a human stance—upright in the dignity of our creation.

There is a vivid image of this posture and what it means for us elsewhere in Luke's Gospel. The Greek word I have translated as "stand up straight" (*anakypto*) is an unusual one. It means literally "to come up out of a bent or crouched position." Luke uses it, earlier on, in the story of a woman who had had a "spirit of weakness" for eighteen years. She had been "bent double and wasn't able to stand up straight at all." Jesus delivered her from this condition, and she stood up straight and glorified God (13:10–13). Being bent double symbolizes bondage for us. Standing up straight signifies the free person. When Jesus freed the woman from her "spirit of weakness," he gave us a symbol of what it means to live a life that is both forgiven and forgiving.

That people can in fact live such a life under the most adverse circumstances seems miraculous to me. No human being should have to rise to such an achievement. Yet it is the most conclusive argument for the power of forgiveness. Persons living under impossible suffering have liberated themselves not only from the weight of past wrongs but even from the terror of present ones by the astonishing expedient of remembering that their oppressors, too, are human.

But to say that this is the highest moment of forgiveness doesn't mean that it is somehow a moral good to remain in a state of oppression. These were people with no true alternatives. For many, there was no escape except death; for others, the only alternative was betrayal of their consciences. This kind of nobility is appropriate only under extreme circumstances. Wherever possible, the first response to abusive situations is to recognize them and work to terminate them.

If in the past we have sometimes encouraged abused spouses or those who were oppressed for their class or ethnicity or race or sexual orientation to forgive each separate incident of wrongdoing, that advice reflected a failure to understand the real dimensions of the issues. The church, the university, the accepted "leadership" of society often show an unreflective tendency to side with the status quo of the moment. Like the religious leaders Jesus challenged, they can and do lose their moral bearings. But the gospel calls for the honoring of all whom God loves. That is the real standard and goal. If we respond only to the individual incidents, they may blind us to the real offense, the offense that keeps people bowed over—which thus remains unconscious, unforgiven, and unredeemed.

Forgiving the Church—and Other Sacred Authorities

One of the difficult challenges some of us face is the need to forgive wrongs done to us by the most sacred figures and institutions in our lives. These include not only the church itself and its clergy but also physicians, therapists, our teachers and mentors, our parents and other kin, and our closest friends. These sacred things and people are images for us of the most holy realities—of God and truth and goodness. When they betray their sacred,

87

sacramental roles and do us harm, either by exploiting us individually or by justifying and sustaining oppressive social structures, the harm is doubled, because at first we may feel cut off from God as well.

It sometimes happens that people who enjoy sacred power, such as clergy and parents and therapists, use that power to extract something from us that they want, whether adulation or inappropriate gain or sexual favors or anything of value. When sacred power is used in this way for personal gain, its whole foundation is compromised. It is no longer transparent to the holy. Since we don't always distinguish clearly between God and religion, we may feel that we've been denied access to God or to whatever good we sought through these sacred persons.

It also happens, at times, that the responsible authorities are so concerned for public appearances that they fail to respond to legitimate complaints. This compounds the problem by creating a deep distrust of all sacred institutions. Where, then, do we go to seek wisdom and life? If you have been betrayed by those whom you thought you could most surely trust, where next will you repose your trust?

The same problems sometimes take on a more social or institutional form for minority groups and those who have less social power. They may find the church and other prestigious institutions siding with the people who would exclude and oppress them. For example, many white-dominated churches supported slavery in the mid-nineteenth-century United States—and then did the same for segregation and other ways of oppressing African American people after their emancipation had put an end to slavery. Many women have found the religious institutions of our society and also such idealistic professions as medicine and the academic world to be major bulwarks of sexism and patriarchy.

Those of us who are gay or lesbian may find ourselves in a particularly difficult spot, having been taught by our churches and our families that we should despise who we are. Even as we come to recognize our affections as gifts received from God, churches often want to treat them as at best a mistake, or at worst an affront to the God who made us. Lesbians and gay men thus find themselves forced to choose between God and church.

How is one to go about forgiving the wrongs of sacred institutions or of individuals who hold sacred trust? The first step is to learn to distinguish between the sacred image and the holy reality it signifies. The church is not God. Clergy are not God. The therapist is an image and at best an agent of mental health, but not an incarnation of it. Even our parents and spouses and friends are people as limited as we are—perhaps, in some cases, more so.

The first step, then, is to overcome our tendency to commit what the scriptures call "idolatry," the habit of confusing the image with what it signifies. It isn't God who has betrayed us, and those who have betrayed us are human like us, even if they may have claimed to be more—even if we may, at times, have asked them to be more and wanted them to be more and treated them as if they were more.

The second step is to understand that all our experience is a mix of good and evil. The fact that a person or institution has harmed us doesn't automatically mean that every aspect of our relationship with the party was evil. In the case of the church, the same institution that justified the oppression that was slavery was also teaching slaves to read about the Exodus from Egypt and so was reinforcing their hope for freedom. The same church that too often sits in arrogant judgment on every marginal group is also the institution that unwittingly keeps subverting itself by reading the message of Jesus aloud in its services of worship.

The same is true with our parents. Even those of us who may have been harmed rather deeply by our parents also owe them our existence. It may never be easy to reconcile these two realities with each other, but even the sense of unease and distress that their conflict creates is a sign that God's work of loving and forgiving can never be completely defeated in this world. Even those who have sought to harm us could not avoid giving us some little scrap of good as well.

We somehow need to retain the power of the sacred to introduce us to holy realities even while we acknowledge that sacred people and institutions are only pale reflections of those realities—and may sometimes even betray them. This calls for a kind of spiritual growth that will bring us, more and more, into our own continuing relationship with God. Given this growth, we won't need to confuse any earthly authority, however sacred or useful to us, with the truth that resides in God alone.

If we don't pursue this goal, we are likely to find ourselves isolated in the world, uncertain of our connection to God and suspicious of all human expressions of sacredness. And, paradoxically, our sacred institutions, with their long traditions of spirituality, are often our best resource (provided we see them *only* as a resource) for cultivating our friendship with God. The challenge, then, is to let the church (and its equivalents) be such a resource without expecting it to be God.

To forgive the wrongs done to us by sacred authorities is possible only when we return those authorities to the human level—the level to which they actually and rightly belong. As we do that, the wrongs will assume more human proportions and the sacred traditions will again become available to us as we pursue our relationship with the holy reality that is the source of all things.

When Forgiveness is Not Forthcoming—
The Other Side of the Problem

I want to take up briefly one other set of problems: those that arise when forgiveness is withheld. What do you do in a situation in which you have committed some wrong and are refused forgiveness, even after you have sought it with appropriate repentance, humility, and tact, and with genuine openness to make amends? Are you trapped henceforth in the wrong you did and prevented from building a new present and future? We have already said that if you have been wronged, you are free of enslavement to the past. Even if the one who did the wrong is unwilling to be reconciled and to join in the creation of a new future, you yourself can move on. Is there any equivalent opportunity for the person who has done the wrong? Is the door to the future permanently closed until the one who was wronged opens it?

Well, reconciliation cannot be forced. And there is no one-sided reconciliation, as we have already said. Neither party can make the other be reconciled. When we have wronged another, particularly someone important or dear to us, and then have repented and sought forgiveness, we may be deeply distressed by the withholding of the forgiveness and the refusal to move toward reconciliation. But we have to accept this as something that only the person we have wronged can change. Whether that person will make the change and offer what has hitherto been withheld, no one else can determine.

As we have already seen, even the offering of an apology and of restitution doesn't oblige anyone to forgive us; it only smoothes the way and makes the process of forgiveness easier. If our overtures are refused, then we have come to the end of what we can accomplish. There may even be some situations in which we simply cannot offer any apology, not because we are unwilling but because the person we have harmed has disappeared or is otherwise unknown to us, or because raising the issue, even by way of making amends, threatens to do more harm than good to those concerned. (The latter is a relatively rare situation, and we should be wary of using it as an excuse to avoid a confession that might merely be embarrassing to us.)

It is quite possible, then, that we will encounter situations in our lives when reconciliation is impossible because of the unwillingness or unavailability of the person we have harmed. How do we proceed? We began this study of forgiveness with a quotation from William Temple reminding us that true repentance is a change of mind. And I have been arguing that forgiving itself is a kind of repentance or conversion. It's a matter of getting a new mind, of seeing things afresh from a perspective more like that of God, whose very nature is love and forgiveness.

The essential thing, then, in moving from past wrong into

future possibility is the experience of getting a new mind. If we have truly been open to that process of conversion, open to receiving the mind of God, then we become new people—not by abandoning our past but by reusing its fragments in the building of the future. The inability of another to forgive does not have to hinder that process. We can continue to grow and to change and to rebuild even without that person's forgiveness. Why? Because forgiveness is the very nature of God and therefore the rock-solid foundation of all existence.

This is not a doctrine of cheap grace. It is not to suggest that our wrongs make no difference or that we do not need to bother about repentance, conversion, change of mind. It is not to suggest that we have no further need to seek forgiveness or that whether the other forgives us or not is of no consequence. No, we still have to confront the truth of our own acts, with their inadequacy, stupidity, and sinfulness. And we have to acknowledge the limits they place on our lives. But we confront these realities alongside the truth of God's love for us and our continuing ability to change and grow.

God's goodness is pure gift, going radically beyond anything we have earned either by good behavior or by repentance. To take hold of it, we acknowledge how gracious God really is and who we really are that we stand in need of that grace. It is a chance for new life. It is a door to the future. It is a beginning, not an end.

God's love isn't a matter of cheap grace, then. It's simply an acknowledgment that one person's life doesn't come to a screeching halt while another person works to accept grace and to grow in repentance or forgiveness—or both. (For which of us is purely wrongdoer or purely victim?) In the long run, the persistent refusal to forgive is itself a denial of God's love, as we have already seen. God's love makes itself known in forgiving us all. If we seek to have this forgiveness for ourselves while denying it to others, we are undermining its very nature and refusing to associate ourselves with God's work in the world. Forgiveness is part of the forgiver's growth into God.

What, then, must we, the wrongdoers who have repented, do?

First, we must accept the assurance of God's love. Second, we must seek the forgiveness of those we have wronged. And, then, if that forgiveness is withheld, we must forgive the withholding of it and build a future anyway—one that will take into account our new encounter with truth, our growth in spirit. If we continue in such growth, we can hold ourselves ready for reconciliation at some future time. We, too, can hold a door open. We can await patiently the moment when the person we have harmed may rediscover the depth of God's forgiveness and begin to share that gift with us.

In the power of God's Spirit, no good thing is impossible. As Christian people, as those who trust in the good news, we live by hope in what we, with God, can build in the future. We also live with the understanding that God can and will feed us and sustain us wherever we find ourselves. The failure or intransigence of others will not prevent us from living richly and faithfully as we grow toward the kingdom. We can forgive without their asking forgiveness—if we have to. We can repent and build anew without their forgiveness—if we have to.

"The brother or sister is not enslaved in such situations. But God has called you in peace."

"Stand up straight and hold your heads up."

You are free. God's generous life of forgiveness is becoming your life, too.

The Forgiving Spirit

～∞～

The Spiritual Journey of Forgiveness

Some of our problems with forgiving arise, as we have seen, from external circumstances—for example, from the refusal or inability of others to participate in a process of reconciliation. At other times, however, our difficulties arise from within ourselves: We do not want to forgive; we are too angry or too hurt to forgive; we long to see those who have wronged us harmed in their turn; we cannot think of them as belonging to the same human reality as ourselves; we cannot imagine them as loved by God.

How are we to deal with this kind of unforgiving spirit in ourselves? Merely trying harder doesn't help much, for forgiveness, as we have been saying, is not simply a duty to be performed but a change of mind, a kind of repentance, a conversion. It involves change within ourselves. So probably it should not surprise us if we sometimes encounter resistance. We all need to change, for there is no possibility of growth without change. To say that I don't need to change would be tantamount to claiming that I'm perfect in the crystalline sense, that I've arrived at the end of all growth and that, from here on, all change would be decay or erosion. Yet, we do fear and resist change because it always has about it the element of the new and the unknown.

Because forgiveness is something that requires spiritual growth on our part, it belongs to the realm of spiritual life rather than to that of simple duty. Spiritual life always has to do with movement and growth. One common image for the spiritual life is "journey" or "pilgrimage." As people of faith, people of the gospel, we have set out on a journey of discovery by which we trust that God will lead us in due course to a new kind of human and divine community. We get foretastes of that community in the here and now, but we expect its fullness in the age to come.

Now, if many people set out on pilgrimage to a place that is sacred to them, they may wind up at the same spot, but they are probably beginning from many different ones. They will not all follow exactly the same path. Some will come from the east and others from the west. Some will have to cross mountains, others rivers, others deserts or savannas or rain forests. It is always part of the wisdom of spirituality to recognize that even though the approach to God has many things in common for all of us, no two of us begin in exactly the same place or reach the goal in precisely the same way.

We need, then, to pay some attention to our beginning points. Where are you starting from in this matter of forgiveness? In this as in all respects, we lead lives that are distinct and individual. We are not completely distinctive, but we can't be reduced to a single common pattern, either. Some of us find it easy to forgive, others difficult. Any of us may find it easy to forgive at some times and then, for no obvious reason, almost impossibly difficult at others.

The Gift of a Forgiving Spirit

Some people seem to have a kind of gift for forgiving. Such a gift is not to be slighted or taken lightly. The person who receives it may not always be aware of its rarity or value. Because forgiving comes easily to that person, it seems as if it's no great matter. But for the rest of us, it definitely is. We can appreciate just how fine a talent this is—precisely because we don't have it.

Paul wrote at some length about the diversity of gifts (1 Cor. 12–14). He was primarily concerned, at the time, that the recipients of one particular gift (speaking in tongues) seemed to think that their gift was better than that of anyone else. But for many people the problem is the opposite one. Far from taking our own gifts too seriously, we don't take them seriously enough. The gifts given to others may look more attractive to us than our own. We may hanker after them and neglect our own. We may feel that the things we really have to work hard at are more valuable spiritually than the ones that come more easily. Often one of the great spiritual challenges for people of faith is learning to respect the gifts we have been given.

The gifts of God are not just inert objects that we can keep on a shelf and admire from time to time. They call for some response. To appreciate them properly, we have to get to know them and practice with them and make use of them. As with all such gifts, the person who receives the gift of ready forgiveness will probably need some time and experience to learn how to use it well. If we forgive in an offhand and careless way, we may give the impression that wrongdoing is easily dismissed and of no great importance, that the brokenness it introduces into relationships is trivial or easily repaired. Our forgiveness may unintentionally come to look like a kind of denial, a way of saying, "Oh, it wasn't really too important after all." That is no kindness, either to the offender or to oneself.

In any case, the gift of forgiveness is never simply an isolated, individual matter. The gifts of the Spirit are given not so much *to* the person who receives them as *through* that person to the community at large. As Paul says, the gifts of the Spirit are what gives life to the whole body of Christ, the community of faith (1 Cor. 12). There is a diversity of gifts so that everyone has something from God to contribute to the body—and also something to receive through the other members of the body. The person for whom forgiveness comes easily receives that gift not merely for his or her personal convenience but for the welfare of the whole.

If you find it easy, then, to forgive, be thankful for so great a gift, and study in what ways you can place it at the service of the larger community. The ability to see the world in the light of

God's forgiveness is one of the critical gifts that equip a person to be a peacemaker. (We could use more of those in our age!) It's also one of the gifts that a reformer or prophet needs. The prophet who cannot forgive the rest of us for our perennial, insufferable inability to see and act on the obvious may find the word of prophecy turning into a mere inarticulate cry of rage that seldom has much influence on those to whom it is addressed.

The gift of ready forgiveness is given to certain persons so that they can use it constructively for the health of the world around them. The forgiving person, being free of the lingering animosities that drive most of us much of the time, can see fresh possibilities and new ways to share in the building of peace—and can then share that vision with others. This is what used to be called a gift of "edification"; but the word has become too pious to mean much. We might call it, in more modern language, an "architectural" gift, one that helps build the future.

The Burden of an Unforgiving Spirit

When we don't have the gift of ready forgiveness, the challenge to forgive may sometimes seem an insuperable problem. At one or another point in our lives, many of us find ourselves in the difficult and painful situation of being trapped in the memory of past wrongs and unable to turn them loose. We get obsessive about what has been done to us. This distracts us from other interests and responsibilities. We cannot find any peace.

Sometimes this reaction takes the form of a profound sense of hurt eating away at our lives. It may cause us to shrink not only from those who have hurt us but even from the world at large, which we fear may contain other people who will be similarly cruel. Oddly enough, we may find that our sense of hurt is accompanied by a sense of shame and self-reproach. We blame ourselves and say we were fools to get into the situation in which we were mistreated. Or we try to figure out what we did to deserve the mistreatment, even though we may know that it was not our fault at all. Ultimately, our vulnerability to such hurt and shame may even cause us to despise life itself, and we may become suicidal.

In other cases, the problem may take the form of anger—an anger that becomes ingrained, excessive, and destructive. It may overwhelm us with its frequent visitations. It may become so intense and obsessive that it prevents us from living the rest of our lives. It may flare up at clearly inappropriate moments. It may drive us to seek a revenge that even we know is excessive. It may last long after the events that triggered it.

One thing that often fuels such anger is our own refusal or inability to deal with it seriously and openly from the beginning. As Blake says, it is the concealed anger that plants the poison tree. When we can find no acceptable way to express the anger, it smolders for a long time underground, gathering strength and heat before it bursts out in ways that may astonish us. It may then strike at people who had nothing to do with the occasion that originally sparked it. It may exclude all other concerns from our attention so that we can't work or play or love as we would wish. Despite our best efforts, it dogs us long after the occasion for it is over and done with—even after the perpetrator of the wrong is dead. And we cannot shake it off.

At worst, these feelings of hurt, shame, and anger may become demonic. Rather then emanating from our own hearts, they act like some external force that has taken up residence in us and tells us what to feel and think. We become alienated from our own lives by these passions. They acquire an alarming power over us. Instead of a situation in which *I* have feelings of anger or hurt, it is as if personified Anger and Hurt are simply using me as a vehicle for their own ends. I become their agent.

Where do such overwhelming feelings come from? And how are we to deal with them and get free of their tyranny? These two questions are related, for the first step in dealing with the problem is to understand something about its sources. Our subject here is still the spiritual life; it is repentance and conversion—a change of mind and heart. Where are our minds and hearts now? What are they seeing and believing that leaves us vulnerable to these outbreaks of demonic passion? How can we move from that false perspective to one that embraces God's truth, the truth of love and forgiveness?

Emotions—Blessing or Curse?

One reaction to the painful passions is to assume that they are intrinsically bad—even that emotion as such is bad. We try to retreat into another part of ourselves and to create a life that is always calm and reasonable, orderly and predictable, so that sudden spasms of fear and anger won't attack us any more. This is another kind of denial, an interior denial that evils can really touch us: "Yes, I was abused. But I can wall off that part of my experience by giving up all feelings."

Emotions, in themselves, are not bad. Quite the contrary is true: hurt and anger, to the soul, are rather like what pain is to the body. They tell us something is wrong. If emotions seem to run amok in some situations—for example, when anger or hurt overpowers us—the useful response is not to try to abandon the emotions altogether but to live with them intelligently, trying to understand better how they work. Our lives are gifts to us—body, soul, and spirit. None of what God has made is bad in itself.

Sometimes teachers of spirituality have tried to ignore or suppress emotions. They have encouraged people to shed them and to become more purely creatures of mind, spirit, and will. This tendency within the Christian spiritual tradition follows in the footsteps of ancient Stoic philosophy, which was profoundly suspicious of what it called "passion." Because Stoicism still has a powerful (and largely unconscious) influence on modern Christians, it will be useful to spend a moment examining it.

Stoicism saw the kind of tyrannical, demonic, controlling passions I have been speaking of here not merely as extreme instances of emotions but almost as their normal state. Emotions are excessive by their very nature, even if they don't always show their full power. And Stoicism thought that the ideal human person would be a purely rational being, untroubled by such distractions. Accordingly, Stoics saw such emotions as anger or hurt or erotic desire as not really being *part* of us at all; they are things that *happen* to us, things that overwhelm us, things we *suffer* (which is the root meaning of the word *passion*). The goal of Stoicism was to free people from such excess emotional baggage so that they could lead a life of untroubled rationality.

This is an attractive picture in some ways, and there are things to learn from it (a bit more on this later). But there are some problems with it. For one thing, it isn't really the picture of humanity assumed in most of the Bible. The Bible not only assumes that human beings are passionate creatures, it even speaks of God in terms of emotions. God loves, gets angry, sorrows, even experiences regret. The God of the Bible is hardly described as a purely rational being!

Still more to the point, the Stoic picture of a purely rational humanity isn't adequate to the full richness of human experience. The ideal Stoic was "impassive," free of passions. But much of what is most rewarding and highest in human culture is in fact deeply involved with the emotions. We relate to the world we live in as much emotionally as we do intellectually or physically. The things we prize most in our humanity are at least partly products of such emotional involvement. A humanity free of emotion would be a very strange and limited sort of humanity.

The arts, for example, are not purely rational in terms either of their creation or of our response to them. Even the music of Bach, with its "learned" fugues ringing ingenious mathematical changes on carefully constructed themes, works its power on us by speaking to the emotions as well as to the mind. And a painting or a play or a dance performance doesn't wait for us to analyze it critically before it begins to affect us deeply. First we are drawn to it by its emotional power; then we analyze it, partly to understand what its emotional power is and what it comes from.

We relate to the natural world, too, not purely out of intellectual fascination with its often hidden workings but also because it seizes us from time to time by means of intense and passionate

101

response—catching us at some unforeseen moment when the light of the newly risen sun cuts slantingly across the tall-grass prairie, or when a bend in the trail reveals, for the first time, a hidden desert canyon peopled by huge cacti with upraised arms, or when the first crocuses of spring appear through a melted patch in the snow. At such moments, the heart lifts and becomes freer. We experience a kind of self-transcendence in which we seem to pass for a moment out of ourselves to be united with the scene or to perceive the world in a new light—one truer, if also more fleeting, than the daily light that illuminates our ordinary lives.

What is true of the arts and of nature is true also of our interactions with one another. When are they ever based on purely rational motives? Economics traditionally assumes that people will behave rationally in the marketplace, and it is right part—but not all—of the time. And in the other realms of our existence—friendship, love, household, partnership in work or play or love—nothing is possible without our emotional engagement with one another. I do not say that emotion is *all*. The rational, detached, analytical side of our human capabilities is also integral to the formation and maintenance of our human connections. But emotion is a vital, necessary ingredient, even if it is also problematic for us at times.

A passionless life might be neater, but it would also be much thinner and paler and far less filled with delight and hope than the one we actually know. It is an old idea (though not a biblical one) that angels are bodiless beings—pure minds, pure spirits. No doubt, if they are truly made that way, their life is very rewarding for them. But God did not create human beings so. God created us with minds or spirits—but also with bodies and souls. We cannot neglect our full, rich, and varied constitution if we are to live the life God has bestowed on us. Some strands of Christian spirituality have suggested that angelic existence, conceived as pure contemplation, might be a good model for human spirituality. It's not. In fact, it's an impossible and self-defeating model. We are creatures of physical sensation and emotional response as much as we are reasoning, analytical, logical beings.

Hurt, Anger, and Helplessness

This defense of emotion in our human makeup may seem like a bit of a digression. But I haven't abandoned the topic in hand. Our question is how to deal with such emotions as hurt and anger when they have come to dominate our lives and paralyze our wills and make it impossible for us to forgive and to let go of past wrongs and so to get on with the building of the future. We cannot resolve these problems by running away from the emotions. Instead, we must look closer at the way these emotions work in our lives and how they manage, at times, to mushroom out of proportion.

As I have suggested, the emotions of hurt and anger are signs of danger to the soul, much like pain in the body. But, also like pain in the body, they aren't always easy for us to interpret. Some pains, after all, are serious and call for immediate attention. Other pains, like the soreness of muscles after unaccustomed exercise, will go away by themselves and don't signal any serious threat. At still other times, real illnesses in the body may not be accompanied by any pain to give the alarm. The alarm system of pain is only an approximation

We learn, as we grow up, how to distinguish some of the different kinds of pain; and when we are perplexed, we usually seek out a physician. But many of us are taught, as children, *not* to pay attention to our emotions—to regard them as childish, as something to grow out of. If we are "good" learners, we may come to a point where we actually have little notion what we are feeling much of the time—particularly at moments of crisis. For men in our world, this state of having no feelings is often held up as an ideal. And the last thing many men would want to do is to consult someone else about feelings they aren't supposed to have in the first place.

But the feelings don't go away—nor do the underlying realities they're trying to tell us about. In the case of hurt and anger, these emotions touch on something very basic to our human condition—the fear of being powerless. Of course, we are all, to some extent or other, powerless. Even if we could get control of the daily details of our lives such that we need never experience any major disappointments (and has that ever really happened to a human being?), our power still stops short in the face of death.

Being human involves being finite: it means having boundaries in space and time. Yet our minds have a kind of unbounded, unlimited quality. We can imagine being much grander and freer than we are. We can imagine a life without suffering or disappointment. But we can't *live* it. And we all have to encounter and deal with that disappointment. It's a profoundly distressing experience, and it begins at least as early as age two, when we begin to rebel against the limits of our control.

We are limited not only by death, by sickness, by failure, by space and time, by the finitude of our own strength and understanding, and by the existence of God, but also by the existence of other people. That is a particularly difficult limitation to deal with, for what limits us in this case is also the thing that makes life worth living! The alternative to being limited by the existence of other people is to be totally singular and to live in complete isolation. Much of the time this tension isn't a serious problem for us, but it becomes a problem if someone attacks us or even harms us inadvertently. We have to have other people—and other people may harm us.

Such attacks, intentional or not, create a sense of danger and need. The soul brings that reality sharply to our attention through the emotions of hurt and anger. Sometimes we quickly find a way to counter the danger, and the emotions dissipate. At other times, the force that threatens us seems impossible to respond to. It is too overwhelming or too amorphous or too ubiquitous. Or it may be backed up by physical force so that we cannot resist, or by venerable authority so that we are unsure, at least for a time, whether it would even be right to resist. Or it may threaten someone or something so precious to us that we feel we have no choice but to submit.

In short, we wind up with a sense of helplessness that prolongs the original harm. The warning emotions of hurt and anger then have no way to resolve themselves. Because the cause of the pain has not gone away, neither do the painful emotions that warned us about it. Instead, they swirl around in our hearts and souls, becoming steadily more toxic and dangerous. The emotions cannot dissipate because we are convinced that we are helpless victims, that we have no meaningful recourse, that we are trapped permanently in a state of harm to ourselves.

This is not a rare or even a surprising situation. Nor is it one to be dealt with lightly. Sometimes, it becomes a central issue in our relationship with God, the world, and ourselves. Think, for example, of the person who was abused as a child by an older relative, perhaps even a parent. In many ways, the child is genuinely helpless. The older relative is bigger and stronger. The sense of dependence on the parent or on the broader household is so great as to preclude either effective self-defense or escape. All the authority of the sacred surrounds the evildoer, too. There seems no alternative but to take what is dealt out, no matter how destructive it may become.

It won't be surprising if this experience of helplessness and fear still pervades life long afterward. The child may grow up to be quite successful and powerful in the normal adult meaning of those terms—yet may remain, at heart, imprisoned by the painful emotions that were triggered in childhood and that have never found any release. The power we have as adults doesn't always make up for the weakness we felt as children.

But the sense of helplessness may not originate in childhood. It can strike us at any time in our lives. Abuse of the vulnerable doesn't just happen to children. It can happen in marriages, in working relationships, through crime, through carelessness, through struggles for political power, because of economic "adjustments" (whether unavoidable or merely callous), in war, in genocide, in slavery (yes, still in the modern world), or through failures of justice. The list is practically endless; it includes all the wrongs we have invented to inflict on one another from the beginning of the human race until now.

105

It is not surprising, as a result, if human beings fall prey to demonic forms of hurt and shame and anger. It's only surprising if there is anyone who *doesn't* do so at some time in life. That would be a true gift of grace. At some point in our human existence, almost all of us will feel vulnerable, helpless, completely blocked off from safety, from love, from whatever is particularly important to us. If the situation continues for long, our souls can become poisoned.

Sometimes we can link this poison directly to its cause in some past harm, though we may not know why it is precisely that incident and not some other that has occasioned so much anguish. At other times, the poisoned emotions seem to take on a life of their own, quite apart from any original occasion. They contribute to a depression that darkens all our days, or they manifest themselves as a free-floating and unpredictable hostility. We find ourselves without the gift of hope to lure us into the future. Or we take offense so often, so easily, and so unpredictably that we wind up alienating those who are dear to us and isolating ourselves. Whatever the exact form our poisoned emotions take, they are likely to have a destructive effect on our lives, both in the turmoil that they create within us and in the way they separate us from the world and the people around us.

Love, Death, and Resurrection

What does the gospel say to this situation? Is there help for us in the message of God's love and forgiveness when we get bogged down in this particular morass? Yes, but it may not be exactly the help we wish for. It is not a specific, direct path out of our state of passion. If we are looking for a patented remedy for hurt or anger, a spiritual pill that will immediately make us feel better, then we are out of luck. The life of the Spirit doesn't work that way.

The life of the Spirit is about growing into our true maturity, the maturity appropriate to us as human beings. There is no shortcut to that goal—no more than there is a shortcut to take us from childhood to adulthood. We get from infancy to maturity only through growth and change—through the frustrations, disappointments, satisfactions, and achievements that go into creating our new perspective on the world. Step by step, an adult perspective replaces that of childhood. Step by step, the perspective of spiritual maturity replaces the perspective of the poisoned emotions.

What the gospel offers is not a quick fix but an opportunity to adopt a new mind, a perspective that respects the limitations by which our lives are bounded and yet also sees beyond them. It offers us a way to take both our power and our limits seriously, a way to achieve some honest hope without covering up our helplessness or hiding from it. The gospel talks about a kind of strength that does not lose its power, even in weakness.

The crucifixion of Jesus is both the greatest scandal of Christian faith and its greatest attraction. It is a scandal to claim that God's nearest approach to humanity resulted in our rejecting and killing the one who embodied God. It proclaims failure: the failure of humanity to respond to God, the failure of God to evoke from human beings the desired response. It looks very much like a dead end.

Yet the surprise of the cross—its astonishing attraction for us— is that the love that brought God to this point of surrender and death refused to back off and give up, even in the face of failure. Failure?! Can God fail? Yes. After all, God has been limited, too, since the moment of creating us. God created us for love, but nothing can compel us to love God in return, because forced love is not love. Even God can fail now—and did fail, on the cross. Yet the love is still hanging there, still offering itself, still forgiving, still eternally seeking us in the hope that we will repent and get a new mind and join in building the future in cooperation with God.

The resurrection of Jesus doesn't negate the pain and loss experienced in the crucifixion. It isn't a *denial* of the cross. The risen Jesus still bore the marks of his suffering (John 20). But the love that brought him to the point of death turned out to be so powerful that even death could not take its life-giving power away. Love can be stymied, yes. It can be rejected; the beloved one can refuse to answer God's courtship with love. But love cannot finally be defeated. It can lose all the battles; but it cannot lose the war. Why? Because it is the source of life, and it cannot lose its own giving, abounding, overflowing nature. Wherever it goes, it makes the world new.

What does this mean for us as we struggle with the entanglements of hurt and anger and grope our way toward spiritual maturity? As I said before, the answer isn't a simple spiritual pain pill that will make us feel better immediately. If you think you have found such a pill, beware! It will turn out to be a dangerously addictive narcotic—something that will eventually kill your spirit as the price of making you feel better for now. Instead, the gospel is an invitation to see the world honestly but from a new perspective, to adopt a bit of God's mind, to keep open the possibility and hope that the past can eventually be redeemed by love because forgiveness can transform even the worst wrongs into building materials for the new world of the future.

Our helplessness afflicts us as an inability to achieve what we desire and feel we need. The limits of human existence are real. God's love doesn't change that. Jesus *did*, after all, die on the cross, and Christianity is no sunny religion of "You can have anything you want if you just ask for it in the right way." (There have been plenty of efforts to turn it into something more upbeat and marketable, but they don't work for long. They keep colliding both with scripture and with reality.) The path to the resurrection leads through the grave.

The gospel doesn't ask us to deny or evade our human limits. Instead, it asks us to look for the power hidden within our weakness, to discover the power of being a human being who is loved by God, sustained by the source of all life, and invited to participate in the creation of a new world. The closer we draw to the source of all life, the more we find that we are far from helpless. In the long run, we cannot be defeated, because our deepest desire is to love, to be associated with God in the joy of God's love, the community of God's household, and the creating of the age to come.

Realism and Hope

This may not, of course, be precisely the message we were hoping to hear. What we initially want to hear is that we will be protected from the people who have harmed us or perhaps that we will be avenged and our own vision of the world we would like to live in will be realized around us. At an extreme, we all still harbor somewhere within ourselves our infant longing to be the absolute center of all reality, to be fed, clothed, changed, bathed, warmed, cuddled, and loved entirely on our own schedule and to our liking. Even after we let go the extreme version of this primal yearning, we still hanker after a world free of serious resistance, a world in which everything would go precisely to our liking with minimal effort on our part.

The problem with that longing is that such a world would ultimately prove unendurably flat and boring. It has two fatal flaws: one is that it would be limited by the scope of my own single and finite imagination, since I would have the whole power of shaping it; the other is that it would have no exchange of love in it, since there would be no other free person able to evoke my love or to answer it. Even God seems to have found such a prospect insufficient. God's love has poured out into the creation of beings (us) who can actually say "no" to God. For only such beings are also capable of saying "yes" and entering into communion with our Maker.

Still, we begin by wanting that infantile fantasy, and we may understandably be put off by a message that says, "Get real! There is real suffering in this world. You will be disappointed more than once. You will suffer at the hands of fate, of nature, of other people. How are you going to live with that?" The message may become even less attractive when we discover that the messenger who embodied it died on a cross.

Yet Jesus was not trapped in the torrent of hurt and anger that you and I sometimes get trapped in. He had every bit as much reason to get stuck there as we do, yet he kept his freedom. The spiritually mature human being isn't spared the troubles that the rest of us encounter. Such a person simply evaluates them differently, sees them from a different perspective, and interprets them in the context of building a more truly humane future. Thus, the harm suffered can come to mean something new, and one's reaction to it changes.

All of us have to face the reality that we cannot change the past *as past.* We cannot make it all turn out right after the fact. Our passage through time, however, is continually opening new possibilities, even in the most hostile of circumstances. We have new opportunities to build the present and the future out of the fragments of the past. Even if we cannot change the external circumstances, we can become new people in relationship to them.

Here is the power that lies hidden in the midst of our apparent helplessness. It is God's power to "make all things new"—a power in which God invites us to share. It takes many forms, but principal among them is forgiveness, which is really a great act of creation, of redefining the past, of changing its meaning as we shape the future. Far from being helpless, the person who forgives is taking charge of the situation and imposing on it a new interpretation.

Suffering and Growth

How can we dare have power in helplessness? Doesn't the power in the situation belong to the one who wronged us—who in fact used power to wrong us? Yes, the power belongs to that person—until, with God's help, we take it for ourselves and for the life of the age to come. We take it by recognizing that no one has the power to deprive us of God's love and friendship. We take it by recognizing that no one can deprive us of our citizenship in the age to come. No one can compel us to be less than what, by God's grace, we truly are.

This doesn't mean that we can sort out all the details neatly and make past wrongs come out right on a one-for-one basis. There may be particular goals in our lives that we eventually have to surrender, particular relationships we cannot mend, particular losses that we simply have to accept. If Jesus wanted to transform the world through economic or political or religious might (and Matthew and Luke tell us that he was at least tempted to do so), he had to surrender that aim. It wasn't easy to take the slower, deeper route of spiritual renewal; but his surrender opened the door to a kind of influence over the world that was far greater than that of any emperor, ancient or modern. Giving up one avenue meant turning to another and better one.

Part of what is happening to us, then, as we pursue the path of forgiveness, is an ongoing education of the emotions and a continuing revision of our perspective on our world to bring it closer to God's. We are learning which goals are realizable and which are not, which goals are of fundamental importance to us and which ones, even if they have seemed intensely attractive, may not really have much permanent value for us.

This is the point at which our Western Stoic tradition becomes useful for us. One of the things the Stoic philosophers perceived is that our desires are often fleeting and poorly grounded. This is something we're all aware of. It is most obvious in childhood, when we're growing rapidly and may quickly lose interest in the toy that fascinated us only a few months before. But the process doesn't come to a halt with adulthood. It's become a commonplace that people in their forties often find that their sense of what is really important undergoes a radical shift. As I've grown older, I find that the process doesn't end at fifty, either. We keep right on reassessing and reevaluating our beliefs and goals, deepening our understanding of them if not always making radical shifts.

Because we are changing and growing, we sometimes find that what seemed a great loss or harm in the past turned out to be the foundation for some subsequent good. The course I didn't get into led me to substitute another one that set me on a different track. The job I failed to get led eventually to a new career. The terrible crisis at work woke us all up to dangers we had been ignoring. The harm done to me led me to be more aware of the ways I may harm others.

I do not mean to sketch some foolishly optimistic scenario.

The suffering, the limits, the vulnerability—these are all real. God suffered them in full in Jesus. There are moments in our lives when we cannot see over the edge of the pit we find ourselves in, times when we can only hang on and try to survive. I don't want to slight or dishonor that reality and the courage that gets people through it. I only mean that suffering, however profound, is not the final word. There remains the possibility of a life beyond it that's informed and enriched by it.

Our plans and expectations for ourselves are not usually the ultimate blueprint for our future. Our lives emerge out of the give-and-take between us and the rest of the world, between our own initiatives and the way external reality prompts us, contradicts us, limits us, stymies us, pushes us in new directions. Ultimately, through all this, God gives us new life. Going directly along our chosen path is not necessarily the best way to become a mature person—and is seldom an available option in any case.

What the Stoics saw, then, was that much of what we perceive as harm done to us is imaginary. It is not harm so much as simply the bouncing back and forth that defines life in the world. Or if it is harm, it is harm done to the person I thought I wanted to be, not to the person I have in fact become—a product of both the opportunities and the troubles my life has seen. Our troubles are typically a stepping-stone toward spiritual maturity, not a barrier to it.

I don't wish to oversell Stoicism. It isn't the gospel. The gospel can in fact say something much more positive here. But as a kind of first level of reflection on our situation, the Stoic perspective is useful. It's useful to ask ourselves exactly what harm we suffered and why we interpreted it as harm. Was it harm to my maturing as a spiritual being? Or was it something more incidental, albeit serious in its own way: harm to my status? to my reputation? to my income? to my health? If so, it may sometimes happen that these apparent harms help us redirect our attention toward becoming spiritually mature. People have at times even pronounced themselves grateful for their losses—if they feel those losses led them to cultivate something of more enduring human value in their lives. With the Stoics, we may find that there is less to forgive than we originally thought.

The Delight of Forgiveness

But the gospel takes us a step further. It takes hold of us even in the midst of our worst distress and says to us, "You are still God's friend, God's beloved. You are still a citizen of the age to come. You are still part of the redemptive process of building a new world. Do not be afraid. You are not helpless. The Jesus who died on the cross lives by the power of the age to come. The love that created you and forgives you is shaping you for that age."

This apparently helpless you who has been hurt badly and has much cause for anger—this helpless you is still a member of God's family, a child of God's household, a free citizen of the kingdom. To stand up straight with the dignity of a free person, to refuse to cower before either present wrongs or past ones, to surrender the goals that have momentarily been stymied and to find new ways of seeking the ultimate goal of new creation—this is what it means to be growing toward spiritual maturity.

And nothing can stand in your way. The God who loves you will not permit it. However insignificant or helpless or shamed or defeated you may feel because of the wrongs done to you, you are even now being courted by the Source of all that is, the Love that made all worlds. You are being wooed. You are being asked for your love in return. God says to you,

> Ah, you are beautiful, my love:
> ah, you are beautiful;
> your eyes are doves. (Song of Sol. 1:15 NRSV)

No helplessness, no failure, no weakness can make you seem less than completely desirable in the eyes of God. You are God's friend, God's beloved, the one for whom God was prepared to give up life on the cross.

And therefore you can afford to forgive. You can afford to be generous, even magnanimous. Have you been at all diminished? No, you are a citizen of the age to come. No harm done to you can come between you and the love of God. No harm can keep you from growing up into the kingdom. No harm can deprive you of that spiritual maturity which stands at the height of human experience.

And what is that height? We can speak here only in images, of course; none of us has really seen the goal yet. One traditional image of heaven is that of an ecstatic, intellectual vision of the One God. If that image gives you delight, then stick with it. It will serve you as long as it evokes delight. For the delight itself is the key. For many—perhaps most—of us, other images may serve better: images that speak of love, of the security of being wrapped in a lover's arms, of the delight of meeting again a long-lost friend, of the life-giving power of what is beautiful and true. Isaiah writes of the age to come as a great picnic in the mountains (Isa. 25). Whatever your image of heaven, let it be flooded with joy and delight. Nothing less is worthy.

There is a hymn that begins, "All my hope in God is founded," and buried in the middle of this hymn is the phrase "Pleasure leads us where we go." Pleasure? Yes, pleasure; beauty; delight; love; friendship. It may seem a little surprising, given that Christianity has so often emphasized duty over pleasure. But it is the ancient teaching and it is true.

We do not go to God, finally, because we should, but because we want to, because we are *drawn* with pleasure and delight to all that is good and true and beautiful. As we move toward God, we shall find that we have less and less need to carry with us a lot of baggage filled with anger and anxiety about old wrongs that cannot, in any case, keep us from the true and lovely God.

It takes too much energy to go on being angry, to go on dwelling on past harms, when I want to be rejoicing in my beloved's beauty, in my friend's companionship. Eventually, I will want to free myself for that delight by abandoning the distractions that have kept me entangled with an unrenewed, unredeemed shadow of the past.

This is how the gospel, the good news, eventually delivers us from an unforgiving spirit. It doesn't work by admonishing us, "You *must* forgive or I won't love you." It doesn't work by providing spiritual wonder drugs. It doesn't work even by training us in forgiveness as such. It works by overwhelming us with love, by drawing us toward the One who loves us and toward the community of the new age. It rebuilds death into resurrection. It drives out hurt and anger by means of pleasure, joy, delight, love, life.

Forgiveness and the Life of Faith

❧

Habitual Forgiveness

W e can think of each act of forgiveness as separate and distinct. When we are faced with a particularly difficult
challenge to forgive, that's exactly how we usually do
think of it. It's a specific problem to be resolved. But we've also
been speaking of forgiveness as intimately linked with the life of
faith and love, as a fundamental part of who we are becoming by
the gift of God's grace. Forgiveness, then, isn't just a series of
actions; it's a way of life.

In Matthew 18:21–22, Peter asks Jesus how often he must forgive his "brother." He plucks a fairly high number out of the air:
"As often as seven times?" Jesus answers, "Not seven times.
Seventy-seven times." Unless your bookkeeping skills are a great
deal better than mine, you won't find it a helpful response. Not,
that is, if you are thinking of each moment of forgiveness as a distinct and separate act. For the real point of the saying seems to be
that we should give up that practice. It is as if Jesus said, "Just
make a habit of it."

The habit of forgiveness isn't usually easy. It may be particularly difficult for those of us who are religious people, who make
some effort to govern our lives according to high ideals, who have
invested time and energy into living according to the rules of
righteousness. I suppose that's why Jesus also stresses the importance of not judging one another: "Don't judge! That way you
won't be judged, either"; "With the measure you use in dealing

117

with others, your own judgment will be measured out"; "Why do you offer to get the speck of dust out of your neighbor's eye and never notice that you've got a whole log in your own?" (cf. Matthew 6:1-5).

Why are we religious folk so quick to judge? It comes down to the same business we have run into before. It's very nice of God to forgive us all, but we'd really rather have our individual excellence recognized instead. We like being in the right. We like at least thinking we're in the right. We don't always like all this rather indiscriminate and extravagant forgiveness that God spreads around.

Strangely enough, our own virtues can be one of our most serious temptations—not because there's anything wrong with being virtuous, but because we would rather rely on them than on God. The medicine for this particular illness is to recover a sense of our own weakness and God's unbounded goodness.

The true saint has a strong sense of shared human weakness. The true saint may indeed be far more virtuous than the rest of us but doesn't feel that's terribly important in comparison with the love of God that we all share. Such a one can forgive more easily. Righteousness is indeed a good thing, as we've said several times. Our world suffers from a lack, not a surfeit, of honesty, integrity, generosity, self-restraint, and even plain civility. But true saints wear their virtues lightly, conscious of their humanity, conscious of what they share with the rest of us rather than what divides them from us.

Forgiveness and Justice

In the long run, our growth in forgiveness is a part of our growth in faith. We can't sever them from each other. As we grow in faith, we experience the change of mind and heart that brings us closer to what God has always aimed for us to be: citizens of the age to come, beloved friends to God and to one another, people whose lives overflow with God's love, people who practice justice and peace.

It may seem odd to connect forgiveness and justice. Sometimes we even think of forgiveness as a way of nullifying justice or of making an exception to it: "Yes, justice demands that you be punished, but I forgive you instead." This has something to do with the way we usually think of justice. We think of it in terms of retributive justice, a process that will punish wrongdoers and balance things out again. Ideally, it will even restore things to their original state, make up for past wrongs, and bring us all back to a perfectly equal starting point. Forgiveness doesn't seem to help us toward this goal. It only muddles the accounts.

This kind of justice has an important role to play in human society. But the idea that it will—or even can—move us toward a truly just society, the life of the age to come, merely by measuring up all past wrongs and correcting them one by one is naive. To choose an extreme case, what would be the chances of accomplishing such justice in the former Yugoslavia, where every ethnic group seems to have a rich record of both sinning against its neighbors and being sinned against? If you want to punish all the culprits and compensate all the victims and settle all the legitimate grudges (not to mention the illegitimate ones), you'll have quite a tangled history to unravel. At times, you might well find yourself punishing and rewarding the same persons.

The idea that we can make things feel as if the wrong never took place is futile. That doesn't mean that it's a mistake to pursue retributive justice; there's a real need for human communities to take a hard look at the truth of the past and to acknowledge the evils in it. But what this kind of justice can accomplish is always limited. It may help clear the ground, but it doesn't do much to build the future. Forgiveness does sometimes dispense people from that particular kind of justice. Forgiveness means, among other things, that we've recognized the ultimate impossibility of putting the past fully "right." The past is over as event, even though it still lives with us in its consequences and in our memories. We cannot make it right. Instead, we can choose, as we go on with life, to reuse the past in creating a new future.

But there is another conception of justice, one in which

forgiveness has a great role to play. This vision of justice focuses not on the past but on the future—on building a just future characterized by peace, by shalom, which means not mere absence of conflict and harm but positive well-being, a world in right relationship. A world characterized by this kind of peace will be a supremely just world, because each person will be taken seriously.

The life of faith aims to produce people who are just: "What does the Lord require of you / but to do justice and to love kindness, / and to walk humbly with your God?" (Mic. 6:8 NRSV). Sometimes the ancient Hebrew or Greek words involved are translated into English as "righteous" rather than "just," but "righteousness" can sound too narrowly individual, too interior, too much a matter of keeping one's nose clean, whereas "justice" captures the social element that is very much a part of this virtue.

The true saints are not simply those who have walked humbly with their God but those who have also done justice and loved kindness. They have lived with a profound and loving respect for others, a respect that freely accords to each person the right to be as much a human being and as much loved by God as they are.

Forgiveness, as we've been describing it, is virtually the same thing. It works by maintaining a basic sense of community with the rest of the human race and by looking forward, even when there is little encouragement from the data, to a time when others will join us in God's household for the creation of a new world. Justice seeks the world of shalom, the life of the age to come. It will do nothing that would make such a world impossible. It will do anything that might actually bring it closer. It will even forgive. Instead of dedicating ourselves, then, to the impossible task of getting the past right, we find ourselves freed by forgiveness to live fully in the present and to begin building something new and better.

The Authority to Forgive

Such a life and such an undertaking are not for weaklings. But then, God has not made us weak. Even if you have succeeded in imagining yourself a powerless person, the true strength given you in creation and in God's ongoing love remains. It only awaits your permission to awake again.

As we have seen, Jesus, in Luke's Gospel, enabled the paralyzed woman to stand up straight again and, in related words, encouraged his disciples to meet the end of the world by standing up straight and holding up their heads. We are that woman. We are those disciples. We are the people to whom that message is given. It is time for us to come out of whatever crouch we have been in—whether a defensive crouch designed to ward off impending blows or an offensive one designed to gather momentum for attack. It is time to stand up like free people, no more and no less.

This is the proper posture for forgiveness. We can't cultivate the power to forgive if we try to remain exactly as we were in all other respects. It won't work. The person who can forgive freely is the citizen of the age to come, a person transformed and renewed by forgiveness and by a life of love and friendship with God.

In John's Gospel, Jesus meets his disciples after his resurrection and gives them the authority to forgive. "As the father sent me," he tells them, "I, too, send you." Then John tells us that he breathed on them and said, "Receive Holy Spirit. If you let go the sins of any, they're released for them; and if you hold on to the sins of any, they are retained" (20:21–22). John doesn't present this as some special ministerial privilege Jesus was giving the disciples. In fact, John never talks about a separate, authoritative ministry in the church. Instead, Jesus is commissioning all who love him. We—all of us—have the power and authority to forgive effectively.

How did we get that power? We got it by having the Spirit of God breathed on us. And that Spirit is God's forgiveness of *us*. Once you've gotten to know forgiveness as a recipient of it, you also begin to learn how to give it. You know how to hand it on. God's forgiveness, of course, was always there, waiting to be received. What we gain by accepting it ourselves is the authority of genuine experience.

It's not only the experience of having heard God's forgiving message that equips us, it's also the experience of our own reluctance and resistance. You know how difficult it can be for some

121

of us to open up and receive God's loving gift and to let go of our profound need to make it on our own. You know how and why we go on maintaining higher standards than God, no matter how destructive it is for us. You know what it is to be so deeply in denial about our lives that we can't admit needing forgiveness, even when it is the thing we most deeply crave.

Our lives and experience, then, actually give us the power and the authority to convey God's forgiveness to others. We receive this power through our own wrestling with God and our assent to God's love. For that love is so great that God invites us to share God's life and work, to cooperate in the great work of forgiveness, the transformation of this world into the life of the age to come. By being forgiven and by forgiving, we become children of God, members of the royal family, God's intimate friends and confidants.

Perhaps this language seems a bit exalted. Perhaps you think that only people who are perfect deserve such titles. Not so. Being a friend of God doesn't mean being omniscient or infallible. The saint remains genuinely human—uncertain, limited, perhaps quite bumbling and inept, like Peter. Saints aren't filled with their own virtue, their own righteousness. They wear that very lightly and are almost unaware of it. They're filled, rather, with God's love as a gift to share with others. They possess a strange and powerful certainty about that one thing. Their certainty is the ultimate power—the power to build the age of justice and peace.

Growing in Faith and Forgiveness

There is no quick and easy answer, then, to the question how we grow in forgiveness, because it is really a question of how we grow in God's grace—how our entire lives are being reshaped, little by little, into the freer and more mature life of the age to come. If we knew either the goal or the way perfectly, it would imply that we had already traversed the way and reached the goal. As it is, we can only remain in an expectant stance and keep growing.

But that doesn't mean there are no guides. We have some

122

models and some benchmarks. We can tell where to begin, and we have at least a general sense of what the goal will look like.

The beginning is to let ourselves start trusting God's love. We are astonished by the miracle of our own creation. We slowly come to accept that God really is wooing us, seeking our love in return, treating us, of all people, as God's best beloved. We accept that we are not in control of this extraordinary event. We didn't make God fall in love with us by being terribly good or even by being terribly repentant. God just loves—and therefore makes us beautiful, almost despite our own wishes at times.

This trusting involves a refocusing (sometimes quite a radical one) of our religious lives. Duty may have been our primary motive before, but now it is the delight and pleasure of discovering grace that stirs us and draws us onward. We find God at work in ourselves and in our lives in surprising ways. We find God drawing us by love and transforming us by love. We receive gifts and share them. We receive forgiveness and hand it on.

To repent means to change your mind, to accept the mind of God as your guide. The greatest repentance for many of us is to discover that we are beautiful in God's eyes—and if in God's eyes, why not in our own, too? We shall find ourselves beautiful not in a possessive or competitive or arrogant way, not in order to show off the advantages we have that others may not have, but simply for the sake of enjoyment—God's enjoyment of us and our enjoyment of God.

Perhaps this sounds more like a goal than a starting point. But we don't have to have any of this down perfectly. We learn it all slowly, step by step. We don't, in fact, have to be completely in love with God and accepting of God's love to become forgiving people. I mean only that this is the voyage of discovery on which we are embarked. It's a long voyage, replete with surprises. We may seem to revisit the same places, both the difficult ones and the pleasant ones, over and over before we really begin to discover God there.

But our ability to forgive arises out of our whole experience of God's love, and it grows as our love of God grows and matures.

We know a little of what it means to be in love with God, even though we are not very far advanced in that relationship as yet. And we know something of what forgiveness looks and feels like, even if we are not yet adept at it.

We might think of the life of forgiveness as a kind of journey whose various stages are marked by familiar signposts. The journey begins with hurt, anger, and hostility. It proceeds, through letting go and the cultivation of a certain habit of kindness, to a state of openness and love. In that state, we can offer forgiveness and reconciliation and the opportunity to rebuild trust (even though we cannot guarantee that they will be accepted).

These are all experiences that we can recognize, even if we cannot automatically or instantaneously reproduce them in our own lives. The journey through them doesn't always proceed in an orderly way. We may take detours. We may circle back through processes we thought we had finished with. We may have to repeat the moment of letting go many times before it proves to have sunk in. But we can at least recognize the steps along the way.

We know that we are growing in forgiveness when we find ourselves starting to draw a freer breath. We find that we have a life to live and that it's focused on God's love, not on the harm done to us. We are no longer defined by that harm, and therefore we no longer wish harm to the person who harmed us. We are even able to wish the offender well—a wish that includes a prayer for that person's change of mind and heart, since it is a change of mind and heart that has brought this good to us.

As we experience this change in forgiving specific harms, we are also forming a habit of kindness in relation to others. Because we are not defined or imprisoned or trapped by the wrongs done to us, we do not have to be touchy or defensive or suspicious of possible slights. Many teachers in the spiritual tradition urge us always to think the best of others. If this is merely a form of denial, it may not be an entirely good idea. But it can be more than that. It can be a habitual way of living in the world that acknowledges the finite character of human existence and is prepared to deal gently with transgressions, our own and those of others.

We may even find that, as we mature in faith, it is harder for people to do us harm. I don't mean that in an external sense. After all, Jesus got crucified. Being a faithful person doesn't give us any guarantee against persecution or other unjust treatment. But the more firmly rooted we are in God's love and the more intimate our friendship with God becomes, the less we shall be anxious about other losses.

The love of God can transform our lives in ways that give them quite different meanings, meanings that cannot be taken away by those who would harm us. Joseph was able to say to his brothers, "It was God who did this." A great many martyrs have been able to pray genuinely and faithfully for their persecutors, even as they suffered and died. How did they do that? Because it was their duty? No. Because they knew themselves loved and gifted and held and forgiven by God.

So are you.

Conclusion

∞

We began this discussion of forgiveness by focusing on conversion—change of mind. That is exactly what forgiveness is for us—taking the risk of conversion, experiencing a change of mind in which we embrace the joy of God's creative love in place of our own hurt and anger and sense of helplessness. God's love makes us strong and rich and able to give and forgive.

Forgiveness is the work not of the weak but of the strong. We forgive not because we are compelled to but because we wish to and we have the freedom to. God's love, working in us, gives rise to the desire to forgive so that we can help build a new world of justice and peace—nothing less than the life of the age to come. The power of God's love works in us to give us the confidence that this can actually happen.

According to some ancient manuscripts of Luke's Gospel, Jesus, at the moment of his crucifixion, says, "Father, forgive them, for they don't know what they're doing" (23:34). This is not a meek or submissive action on Jesus' part. Indeed, despite our pious language about Jesus' passion, there is nothing meek or submissive about the stories of it in the Gospels. Jesus stands up to the authorities as their equal—even their superior—despite all the obvious evidence to the contrary. He is not cowed by them or by the prospect of suffering and death.

There is a moment of submission in the story, of course—in the Garden of Gethsemane as Jesus prays. But it is submission to the will of God, not of human beings. It is Jesus' acceptance of the difficult task of bringing God's love to life in the midst of this world's vicious craziness. Jesus accepted his unwelcome task much as Moses and Jeremiah accepted theirs earlier in the biblical story—reluctantly, but with free consent.

Jesus' prayer on the cross that God would forgive those who are killing him has nothing to do with submission. It is more like the son and heir of a royal family appealing for clemency toward those who have done some wrong. Jesus addresses God directly and without formality as "Father." He plays much the same role here that Jonathan played long before in rescuing David from the anger of Jonathan's father, Saul (1 Sam. 20). The great difference, of course, is that Jonathan was appealing to a frightened, angry, suspicious man who was barely up to the task of kingship, whereas Jesus is appealing to the One who originated the whole great project of forgiveness.

It's a distressing irony that some strands of Christian theology have interpreted the cross as a blood payment designed to buy off God's anger at us. If God was so angry and so determined on punishment, what motivated God to become incarnate in Jesus and to endure the cross in the first place? Yes, God does detest sin, because of what it does to us and indeed to the whole world that God created and pronounced good. But the same love that moved God to create us also leads God to seek us out, to become one of us, even to suffer with us—not to pay some fine on our behalf but to assure us absolutely and beyond any possible denial that God's love is inexhaustible and beyond our fathoming.

The depth of God's love is shown in God's unending capacity to forgive. As far down into God as we shall ever be able to reach, we will find nothing but love. And in whatever is beneath that, in whatever abysses of God there are that we can never plumb, there is nothing but love. From the beginning it is all love: "God is love." And this love is the ultimate, triumphant power that overcomes everything opposed to life: "Love's a man of war."

So Jesus appeals to God with confidence. Jesus is heir to the throne of God's love, that throne which is not only exalted and glorious but is also the true home of the whole created order. He appeals by means of love to the very fount of love. He gives himself by love. He forgives by love. He, too, is love.

Jesus appeals from another vantage point of power, too. He appeals, as the one who knows and understands what's going on, on behalf of people who don't know what they're doing. In his day, these were people who, falling into the worst trap of the religious everywhere, thought they were befriending the God whom they were in fact trying to kill. They didn't understand that in attacking the one who dealt with them truthfully and faithfully, they were attacking the source of their own life. They thought they were killing some stranger—as if that were a trifling matter!— and didn't recognize that they were actually attempting a kind of spiritual suicide.

Does such ignorance make human misdeeds less destructive? No. We can still work great harm to ourselves and others even when we don't really understand what we're doing. But God sees in our ignorance at least a hope that we have not truly *chosen* the evil, that there is something in us that can still respond to love and can grow into the citizenship of the age to come. And so Jesus appeals to God to forgive us so that our ignorance may yet have time to turn into knowledge.

But whether Jesus appeals on the basis of his intimacy with God or on the basis of his wisdom, either way he is bringing his riches and power into play on behalf of those who are wronging him. His forgiveness springs from a royal, a sage, a divine generosity. It is an authoritative act; and the authority behind it is love. It aims not to correct the past nor to punish offenses but to give rise to a new world.

What I've said about Jesus' act of forgiveness from the cross applies also to us. As our friendship with God becomes more intimate, as we become more closely identified with God's good work in the world, we shall become more, not less, forgiving. How strange that in our world, we so often think of the "godly" as rigid and unforgiving. It was exactly that expectation that led the "godly" of Jesus' own time to crucify him. To be truly godly, to be "perfect" as our heavenly Father is perfect, does not mean being rigid and stern. It means scattering our goodwill freely over the deserving and the undeserving alike, over those who need our forgiveness and those who don't.

We are invited, then, to return to the rich embrace of God's family, the family we came from originally but abandoned; we are invited to join God in forgiving the world as part of the great family project to reclaim it and to bring it anew to its longed-for beauty. Only the rain of God's forgiveness will make this desert bloom in its proper and true colors. Only the bounty of God's forgiveness can lure human beings back into love of one another and of the One who made them.

We're also invited to share God's wisdom and understanding, to recognize that love is the ultimate reality. God's goodwill cannot ultimately be defeated. When we resist God's love, we are fighting a flood that will carry us onward anyway. If we *could* kill God, we would extinguish our own life in the same instant. There is no way to live without the source of all life, to prosper without the source of all riches, to love without first being loved. The more firmly we come to be rooted in this wisdom, the easier we shall find it to forgive those who wrong us and to hold open for them the door to the future, the door to the life of the age to come.

God is love. And because God is love, love turns out to be the driving force of all creation and the power that binds us to our first Lover and to all whom that One loves. What was true of God's own first gift is true of our daily existence, too. It is love that makes the creator create. It is love that unites the creation to the one who created it. Love makes friends. Love creates family. Love is the key that unlocks the ecstasy of lovers. Without this great seeking and finding, creation would remain flat and inert. Without it, our lives would become pointless. With it, we truly begin to live.

God's patience in forgiving is a way of courting us, of soliciting *our* love. Our love is the one thing in the world, after all, that

130

God can't command. God can only ask for it. In asking for it, God has been willing to go to great expense and to take great risks. If we answer this love with our own, we shall be united to God. If we take the further risk of loving and forgiving one another, we shall find ourselves in the process of creating a new world, the very life of the age to come, where we human beings will no longer fight each other in our ignorance, destroying all hope of blessing, but will share the fruits of love in a free exchange of understanding and good will.

Love is the powerful attraction that the all-powerful God uses to draw us into relationship with our creator—and with one another. And, at the same time, it is the fulfillment of the relationship into which it draws us. The reward of love is love. Forgiveness merely shows the depth and strength of this love, which is not deflected even by repeated failure nor exhausted even by repeated rejection.

Only the strong can forgive. God, who is strongest, forgives best. But we have been invited to become members of God's household, sharers in God's wisdom and knowledge, people strong with God's strength and generosity. We, too, can join in the infinite exchange of love and forgiveness that opens the door to the future.

The first step is as simple as saying "yes" to the possibilities before us: After Jesus asked God to forgive those who were killing him, a robber being crucified alongside Jesus said to him, "Jesus, remember me when you enter upon your reign." Jesus said to him, "Amen, I say to you, today you will be with me in paradise" (Luke 23:42–43).

Acknowledgments

⚮

This work began as presentations in a variety of church contexts, where my hearers' attentive listening and penetrating observations and questions did much to shape it. My thanks to Christ Church, Alameda, California; Christ Church, Nashville, Tennessee; the Bible Lecture series at Christ Church Cathedral, Indianapolis, Indiana; and (for a bit of variety) Grace St. Paul's Church, Tucson, Arizona.

I profited greatly from the conversation that followed those presentations—far more than I can acknowledge here. I also thank, in particular, the following individuals who have given me significant moments of insight and guidance:

Sue von Baeyer, for stimulating conversations on our morning walks,

Marti Steussy, especially for prompting me to rework my treatment of forgiveness and justice,

Tom Schultz, especially for pointing out to me the importance of choice at the beginning of the process of forgiveness,

Chris Eastoe, for some astute comments about organization of this book,

Bert Herrman, for reminding me of the particular challenge many gay and lesbian people have in forgiving the church,

Hal Rast, for his unflagging support and encouragement,

and **Debra Farrington,** for her good editorial eye.

Translations of New Testament passages are my own. Old Testament passages are drawn from the King James Version (AV) or New Revised Standard Version (NRSV), except for the Psalms, which are quoted from the Book of Common Prayer (BCP) (Episcopal Church in the United States of America 1979).